PORTMEIRION

Book of

Entertaining

PORTMEIRION
Book of
Entertaining

EBURY PRESS
LONDON

Published by Ebury Press for Portmeirion Potteries Ltd,
Penkhull New Road, Stoke on Trent, ST4 5DD

Ebury Press is an imprint of Century Hutchinson Ltd,
20 Vauxhall Bridge Road, London SW1X 2SA

ISBN 0 85223 892 4

Editors: Gillian Haslam and Helen Southall
Designer: William Mason
Photographer: James Murphy
Home Economist: Allyson Birch
Stylist: Sarah Wiley

Filmset in Garamond by Advanced Filmsetters (Glasgow) Ltd
Printed and bound in Italy by New Interlitho, S.p.a., Milan

Contents

INTRODUCTION

The popularity of the *Portmeirion Book of Country Cooking*, published in 1988, has been such that we have been encouraged to bring out the *Portmeirion Book of Entertaining*. In this second book, we give a selection of dishes suitable for buffets, dinner and lunch parties and other festive occasions, formal and informal. We have included many country and traditional dishes like Beef in Stout and Duck with Cumberland Sauce, intriguing eighteenth century favourites Salmagundi and Syllabub, and a whole selection of other interesting and delicious suggestions. How many cooks, for instance, have thought of making Fish Wellington as well as the classic Beef Wellington? With chapters on Brunch and Sunday Lunches, and Starters, Vegetable Dishes, Desserts, Fish, Meat and Afternoon Tea, the book provides an invaluable source of ideas for home entertaining.

To make a party really successful, of course, the food has not only to be good, it has to look good. We at Portmeirion feel that this is our strong suit, and the book's numerous illustrations form a visual primer on the presentation and service of party food. The pictures celebrate Portmeirion's Botanic Garden and Pomona pottery and also the many accessories, placemats, napkins and so on which complement the delicious dishes whose recipes are to be found in these pages. Portmeirion's pottery, placemats, napkins, trays and furnishing materials, all designed by Susan Williams-Ellis, help you to create a party atmosphere.

The book was photographed at Portmeirion in Wales, the famous architectural fantasy village created by Susan's father, Sir Clough Williams-Ellis. Susan and her father share the same creative approach. Both try to open people's eyes to the pleasures of design, whether of buildings and landscapes or bowls and curtains. Both share a fundamental message and Sir Clough's exuberance carries the beguiling suggestion that life ought to be one long party. Susan provides the furnishings and accessories for parties which, if not quite lifelong, are at least enjoyable and to be remembered.

EUAN COOPER-WILLIS

*Right: Tagliatelle with seafood and
champagne sauce (page 40)*

BREAKFAST AND BRUNCH

Champagne Cocktail

Steep the sugar lumps in advance of serving for this cocktail, but do not open and pour the champagne until your guests are ready.
SERVES 4

4 sugar lumps
few drops of Angostura bitters
60 ml (4 tbsp) brandy
60 ml (4 tbsp) fresh orange juice
4 ice cubes
1 bottle of champagne, well chilled
4 twists of orange zest

1. Put one sugar lump in the bottom of each of four champagne flutes. Sprinkle over the Angostura, then put 15 ml (1 tbsp) each of brandy and orange juice into each glass.
2. Put one ice cube in each glass and top up with champagne. Decorate with orange zest.

Mango and Passion Fruit with Sabayon Sauce

If you have an electric whisk, it won't take more than a few minutes to whisk up the sabayon sauce.
SERVES 4

2 ripe mangoes
2 passion fruit
2 egg yolks
50 g (2 oz) caster sugar
150 ml (¼ pint) dry white wine
1 liqueur glass of brandy

1. Peel and slice the mangoes and fan out on four individual plates. Cut the passion fruit in half and scoop the pulp and seeds over the mango. Cover and set aside.
2. Put the egg yolks and sugar in a bowl over a pan of gently simmering water. Whisk with a hand-held electric whisk, rotary beater or balloon whisk until the mixture is thick and mousse-like.
3. Whisk in the wine, a little at a time, then the brandy. Remove from the heat and continue whisking until cool.
4. To serve, uncover the fruit and pour the sabayon around it.

Herrings in Oatmeal

The oatmeal in this dish adds to its bulk and fibre as well as absorbing the rich oiliness of the herrings. Ask the fishmonger to prepare the herrings for you.
SERVES 4

4 medium herrings, cleaned, heads and tails removed
salt and freshly ground pepper
100 g (4 oz) medium oatmeal
30 ml (2 tbsp) vegetable oil
25 g (1 oz) butter
lemon wedges, to serve

1. To remove the backbones of the fish, open them out on a board, cut side down, and press lightly with the fingers down the length of the backbone. Turn the fish over and ease the backbone up with the point of a knife. Fold the fish in half, season well and coat with oatmeal.
2. Heat the oil and butter in a large frying pan and fry the herrings for about 5 minutes on each side. Drain and serve hot with lemon wedges.

Egg Fricassée

The subtle flavour of tarragon gives this creamy egg dish an extra special touch.

SERVES 4

200 ml (7 fl oz) milk

small piece of onion

small piece of carrot

1 bay leaf

6 peppercorns

225 g (8 oz) packet frozen puff pastry, thawed

25 g (1 oz) butter

30 ml (2 tbsp) plain flour

150 ml (¼ pint) soured cream

2.5 ml (½ tsp) dried tarragon, or 10 ml (2 tsp) snipped fresh tarragon

salt and freshly ground pepper

6 eggs, hard-boiled

sprig of fresh tarragon, to garnish (optional)

1. Put the milk in a saucepan with the onion, carrot, bay leaf and peppercorns and bring to the boil. Remove from the heat and leave to infuse for 10 minutes, then strain.

2. Meanwhile, to make the pastry triangles, roll out the pastry to an oblong 25 × 10 cm (10 × 4 inches). Divide lengthways in two and cut each strip into 10 triangles. Place on a baking sheet and bake in the oven at 220°C (425°F) mark 7 for 12–15 minutes or until golden brown and well risen.

3. Meanwhile, melt the butter in a saucepan and stir in the flour. Remove from the heat and gradually stir in the strained milk, soured cream, tarragon and seasoning. Return to the heat and bring to the boil, stirring all the time until the sauce thickens. Simmer for about 5 minutes.

4. Shell and slice the eggs, reserving the yolk from one. Add the egg slices to the sauce and simmer gently to warm the eggs. Taste and adjust the seasoning. Pour into a warmed shallow serving dish.

5. Sieve the reserved egg yolk and use with the tarragon sprig to garnish the dish. Serve accompanied by the pastry triangles.

Smoked Haddock Kedgeree

A classic English breakfast dish of smoked fish in creamy rice, seasoned with cayenne pepper and nutmeg.

SERVES 4

450 g (1 lb) smoked haddock

100 g (4 oz) long grain rice

2 large eggs, hard-boiled, shelled and chopped

30 ml (2 tbsp) lemon juice

pinch of cayenne pepper

pinch of grated nutmeg

150 ml (¼ pint) single cream

salt and freshly ground pepper

50 g (2 oz) butter, diced

30 ml (2 tbsp) finely chopped fresh parsley

parsley sprigs, to garnish

1. Place the haddock in a large shallow pan and just cover with water. Poach for about 15 minutes or until tender. Drain, skin, bone and roughly flake the fish.

2. Meanwhile, cook the rice in boiling salted water for about 15 minutes or until tender, then drain.

3. Carefully mix the haddock, rice and eggs together. Stir the lemon juice, cayenne pepper and nutmeg into the cream and fold into the haddock and rice. Season to taste with salt and pepper. Spoon the mixture into a greased ovenproof dish, dot with the butter and cook at 180°C (350°F) mark 4 for 25 minutes.

4. Stir in the chopped parsley and garnish with parsley sprigs just before serving.

Overleaf: Champagne cocktail (page 8), mango and passion fruit with sabayon sauce (page 8), smoked haddock kedgeree (above)

Poached Eggs with Cream and Parsley Sauce

An attractive pale green sauce, well speckled with parsley, tops carefully poached fresh eggs. A little mature Cheddar gives a lovely taste.

SERVES 4

25 g (1 oz) butter
25 g (1 oz) plain flour
300 ml (½ pint) milk
10 ml (2 tsp) chopped fresh parsley
salt and freshly ground pepper
50 g (2 oz) mature Cheddar cheese, grated
30 ml (2 tbsp) soured cream
4 eggs
4 slices of wholemeal toast

1. Put the butter, flour, milk and parsley in a saucepan. Heat, whisking continuously, until the sauce thickens, boils and is smooth. Simmer for 1–2 minutes, then season to taste with salt and pepper.

2. Remove the pan from the heat, add the cheese and stir until melted. Fold in the cream.

3. Poach the eggs by breaking them into a pan of barely simmering water and cooking for 3 minutes. Lift out with a draining spoon and drain on absorbent kitchen paper.

4. Place one egg on each slice of toast and cover with parsley sauce. Serve immediately.

Breakfast Pancakes

Pancakes are quick and easy to prepare, and good at any time of day. Topped with grilled bacon, scrambled eggs and tomato slices, they make a welcome change from toast.

MAKES 4

25 g (1 oz) plain wholemeal flour
25 g (1 oz) medium oatmeal
salt and freshly ground pepper
4 eggs, beaten
250 ml (9 fl oz) milk
butter, for frying
100 g (4 oz) back bacon, grilled and chopped
2 tomatoes, sliced and grilled

1. Put the flour, oatmeal, salt and 15 ml (1 tbsp) beaten egg into a bowl. Gradually stir in 150 ml (¼ pint) milk and beat to form a smooth batter.

2. Melt a little butter in a 20.5 cm (8 inch) frying pan. When hot, pour in 45 ml (3 tbsp) of the batter, tilting the pan to cover the base. Cook until the pancake moves freely, then turn over and cook until golden. Slide on to a warmed serving plate and keep warm. Repeat to make four pancakes.

3. Beat together the remaining beaten egg, milk and salt and pepper to taste. Scramble in a small saucepan over gentle heat, stirring until the egg starts to set.

4. Place spoonfuls of the egg on to the pancakes, and add the bacon and tomato slices. Fold the pancakes over. Serve warm.

Devilled Kidneys

Kidneys are a traditional brunch dish. They are quick and easy to prepare and make a flavoursome start to the day.

SERVES 4

---

8 lamb's kidneys

15 ml (1 tbsp) mustard powder

10 ml (2 tsp) Worcestershire sauce

50 g (2 oz) butter

salt and freshly ground pepper

4 slices of hot toast

---

1. Skin the kidneys, cut in half and core. Mix the mustard with the Worcestershire sauce.

2. Heat the butter in a saucepan, add the kidneys, salt and pepper, and brown quickly for 2 minutes. Lower the heat, cover and cook very gently for 6 minutes.

3. Add the mustard mixture to the kidneys, stir well and cook slowly for a further 2 minutes. Stir and serve on the hot toast.

Honey and Orange Apricots

This is very easy and quick to prepare. It can be made the day before, and kept in a cool place.

SERVES 8

---

100 ml (4 fl oz) fresh orange juice

30 ml (2 tbsp) lemon juice

50 ml (2 fl oz) clear honey

8 ripe apricots, stoned and sliced

450 g (1 lb) blueberries, stalks removed

---

1. Mix together the orange and lemon juices. Add the honey and stir until it has dissolved. Add the apricots and blueberries.

2. Chill for at least 1 hour before serving.

Oxford Sausages

These sausages are succulent, meaty and well flavoured with herbs and lemon. They are shaped in the hands before frying, and do not have skins.

MAKES ABOUT 18

---

450 g (1 lb) lean boneless pork

450 g (1 lb) lean boneless veal

350 g (12 oz) shredded suet

225 g (8 oz) fresh breadcrumbs

grated rind of $\frac{1}{2}$ lemon

5 ml (1 tsp) freshly grated nutmeg

15 ml (1 tbsp) chopped fresh mixed herbs or 5 ml (1 tsp) dried mixed herbs

5 ml (1 tsp) chopped fresh sage or a pinch of dried sage

salt and freshly ground pepper

1 egg, lightly beaten

plain flour, for coating

---

1. Mince or very finely chop the pork and veal and put it in a large mixing bowl. Add the suet, breadcrumbs, lemon rind, nutmeg and herbs, mix together and season to taste. Add the egg to the mixture and mix well with a fork until all the ingredients are thoroughly combined and bound together.

2. With floured hands, form the mixture into about 18 sausage shapes. Coat each sausage with flour, shaking off any excess.

3. Cook the sausages under a hot grill, turning frequently, until evenly browned and cooked through. Serve with grilled bacon and tomatoes.

Soups and Starters

Devonshire Crab Soup

Crab is a popular choice for entertaining. Here, it helps make this a very special soup to serve at any time of year.

SERVES 6

25 g (1 oz) butter

1 small onion, skinned and finely chopped

1 celery stick, cleaned and chopped

75 g (3 oz) long grain rice

568 ml (1 pint) milk

meat of 1 cooked crab, or 225 g (8 oz) frozen or canned crab meat, drained and flaked

300 ml ($\frac{1}{2}$ pint) chicken stock

salt and freshly ground pepper

5 ml (1 tsp) anchovy essence

30 ml (2 tbsp) brandy

150 ml ($\frac{1}{4}$ pint) double cream

chopped fresh parsley, to garnish

1. Melt the butter in a large saucepan, add the onion and celery and cook for 10 minutes or until soft. Add the rice and milk, cover and cook for 15 minutes or until the rice is cooked. Allow to cool slightly.

2. Pass the soup through a sieve or purée in a blender or food processor. Return to the pan and add the crab meat. Add the stock, seasoning and anchovy essence and reheat.

3. Add the brandy and cream and heat gently, without boiling. Transfer to a warmed soup tureen, sprinkle with chopped parsley and serve very hot.

Left: Honey and orange apricots (page 13)

Turkey and Hazelnut Soup

Cooked leftover turkey works well in this recipe. Just add it to the stock and simmer for 2–3 minutes or until hot. Chopped hazelnuts add a hint of nuttiness and a hearty texture.

SERVES 4–6

75 g (3 oz) hazelnuts

15 g ($\frac{1}{2}$ oz) butter

1 medium onion, skinned and roughly chopped

2.5 ml ($\frac{1}{2}$ tsp) paprika

225 g (8 oz) turkey breast fillet, skinned and chopped

900 ml (1$\frac{1}{2}$ pints) chicken stock

1 egg yolk

150 ml ($\frac{1}{4}$ pint) single cream

15 ml (1 tbsp) chopped fresh chervil or 5 ml (1 tsp) dried chervil

salt and freshly ground pepper

fresh chervil sprigs, to garnish

1. Place the hazelnuts on a sheet of foil and toast under the grill, turning frequently. Put in a blender or food processor and chop very finely.

2. Melt the butter in a saucepan, add the onion and paprika, cover and cook for 5 minutes or until soft.

3. Add the turkey breast and stock and simmer for 5 minutes or until tender. Do not over-cook or the turkey will become rubbery.

4. Allow to cool slightly, then purée in a blender or food processor.

5. Blend the egg yolk with the cream and add to the soup. Return the soup to the pan and reheat without boiling, stirring all the time.

6. Add the hazelnuts and chopped chervil and season to taste. Serve hot, garnished with sprigs of fresh chervil.

Cream of Spinach Soup

You can use frozen spinach leaves or frozen chopped spinach for this simple soup starter.

SERVES 6

50 g (2 oz) butter

175 g (6 oz) packet frozen spinach, thawed

1 medium onion, skinned and finely chopped

25 g (1 oz) plain flour

300 ml ($\frac{1}{2}$ pint) chicken stock

568 ml (1 pint) milk

salt and freshly ground pepper

pinch of grated nutmeg

30 ml (2 tbsp) single cream

1. Melt the butter in a large saucepan and gently sauté the spinach and onion for 5–6 minutes. Add the flour and stir thoroughly, then remove from the heat.

2. Add the stock, then return to the heat and bring to the boil, stirring continuously until the mixture thickens. Carefully blend in the milk and bring back to the boil, stirring. Reduce the heat, cover and simmer for 15–20 minutes. Season to taste with salt, pepper and nutmeg.

3. Pass the soup through a sieve or purée in a blender or food processor. If necessary, thin with milk. Reheat gently.

4. Pour into a warmed soup tureen or individual dishes. Stir in cream just before serving.

Walnut and Mushroom Soup

The addition of walnuts to this creamy mushroom soup gives it a delicious nutty flavour.

SERVES 6

350 g (12 oz) button mushrooms

50 g (2 oz) butter

1 small onion, skinned and finely chopped

15 ml (1 tbsp) plain flour

450 ml ($\frac{3}{4}$ pint) chicken stock

450 ml ($\frac{3}{4}$ pint) milk

50 g (2 oz) walnuts, chopped

2.5 ml ($\frac{1}{2}$ tsp) salt

freshly ground pepper

150 ml ($\frac{1}{4}$ pint) single cream or top of the milk

1. Wipe and chop the mushrooms, reserving a few finely sliced mushrooms for garnish.

2. Melt the butter in a saucepan, add the onion and cook for 5 minutes or until soft. Add the chopped mushrooms and fry for 2 minutes.

3. Remove from the heat and stir in the flour, stock, milk, walnuts, salt and pepper. Bring to the boil, then reduce the heat, cover and simmer for about 30 minutes. Allow to cool slightly.

4. Purée the soup in a blender or food processor, then return to the pan and add the sliced mushrooms and cream. Cook gently, without boiling, for a further 5 minutes. Taste and adjust the seasoning. Serve hot.

Chilled Skate Soup

Only the 'wings' of skate are eaten. Lumpfish roe is a form of 'mock' caviar. True caviar comes from the sturgeon fish.
SERVES 6

450 g (1 lb) skate
1 medium onion, skinned and thinly sliced
100 g (4 oz) celery, cleaned and sliced
45 ml (3 tbsp) lemon juice
2 bay leaves
salt and freshly ground pepper
300 ml (½ pint) milk
150 ml (¼ pint) soured cream
25 g (1 oz) lumpfish roe (caviar-style)
snipped fresh chives, to garnish

1. Rinse the skate and place in a medium-sized saucepan with the onion and celery. Pour over 600 ml (1 pint) water and add 30 ml (2 tbsp) lemon juice, the bay leaves and seasoning.
2. Bring slowly to the boil, cover the pan and simmer gently until the fish begins to flake away from the bone.
3. Lift the fish from the soup and flake it, discarding the skin and bone. Place the fish in a blender or food processor.
4. Add the pan ingredients (discarding the bay leaves) and milk to the fish and purée until smooth. Taste, adjust the seasoning and add the remaining lemon juice, if necessary.
5. Chill well before serving with soured cream and caviar swirled through each portion. Garnish with snipped chives.

Chilled Asparagus Soup

Chilled soup makes an excellent start to a dinner party on a warm evening and this one, with its pretty green colour and luxurious consistency, is a particularly good choice.
SERVES 6

700 g (1½ lb) asparagus
25 g (1 oz) butter
2 medium onions, skinned and roughly chopped
1.4 litres (2½ pints) chicken stock
salt and freshly ground pepper
150 ml (¼ pint) single cream

1. Cut the heads off the asparagus and simmer them very gently in salted water for 3–5 minutes or until just tender. Drain well and refresh with cold water.
2. Scrape the asparagus stalks with a potato peeler or knife, to remove any scales, and cut off the woody ends. Thinly slice the stalks.
3. Melt the butter in a large saucepan. Add the asparagus stalks and onions, cover and cook for 5–10 minutes or until beginning to soften.
4. Add the stock and season to taste. Bring to the boil, cover and simmer for 30–40 minutes or until the asparagus and onion are tender.
5. Allow to cool slightly, then purée in a blender or food processor until smooth. Sieve to remove any stringy particles, then stir in the cream.
6. Cover and chill in the refrigerator for 2–3 hours. Serve garnished with the reserved asparagus tips.

Overleaf: Chicken with tarragon mayonnaise (page 64), chilled asparagus soup (above)

Asparagus with Coriander Hollandaise Sauce

This luxurious first course is enhanced by the unusual addition of coriander to the hollandaise. The asparagus can be prepared for cooking, and the coriander seeds toasted, some time ahead.

SERVES 8

800 g (1¾ lb) asparagus, stalks trimmed and scraped

15 ml (1 tbsp) lemon juice

FOR THE SAUCE

45 ml (3 tbsp) coriander seeds, crushed and lightly toasted

225 g (8 oz) unsalted butter, diced

45 ml (3 tbsp) lemon juice

25 ml (1½ tbsp) white wine vinegar

4 egg yolks

pinch of sugar

pinch of salt

fine strips of lime rind, to garnish

1. Put the coriander seeds and butter in a small saucepan and warm gently until the butter just begins to bubble. Remove from the heat, cover and leave to infuse for 20 minutes.

2. Tie the asparagus into four equal bundles. Stand them in a large saucepan of boiling salted water, to which the lemon juice has been added, packing foil around them if necessary so that they stand upright. The tips should be out of the water. Cover with a lid or dome of foil and cook gently for about 10 minutes or until tender, depending on the size of the spears.

3. Meanwhile, to make the sauce, put the lemon juice and vinegar in a saucepan and bring to the boil. Gently reheat the coriander butter until just beginning to foam. Put the egg yolks, sugar and salt in a blender and blend briefly, then, with the motor running, slowly pour in the lemon juice and vinegar mixture. When it has all been absorbed, slowly pour in the coriander butter, with the motor still running.

4. Drain the asparagus well and arrange on warmed plates. Place a small pool of sauce on each plate. Garnish with fine strips of orange and lemon rind and sprigs of chervil.

Alternatively, the asparagus can be piled on to one large, warmed plate and the sauce served in a warmed bowl for the guests to help themselves. Garnish as above.

Lymeswold with Redcurrant Jelly

Lymeswold is a relatively newly developed English cheese. For this recipe, Brie would be a good substitute, if preferred.

SERVES 4

150 g (5 oz) white Lymeswold cheese

1 egg, beaten

50 g (2 oz) fresh wholemeal breadcrumbs

vegetable oil, for frying

30 ml (2 tbsp) redcurrant jelly

shredded lettuce, to serve

redcurrants and fresh parsley, to garnish

1. Cut the cheese into four slices. Brush with beaten egg and coat with breadcrumbs.

2. Heat some oil in a large frying pan and fry the cheese slices for 10 seconds on each side or until golden. Drain on absorbent kitchen paper. Fry in batches if necessary.

3. Put the redcurrant jelly and 15 ml (1 tbsp) water in a saucepan and heat gently until the jelly melts.

4. Place each slice of cheese on a bed of shredded lettuce on individual plates. Pour over the redcurrant sauce, garnish with redcurrants and parsley and serve at once.

Stuffed Mushrooms

This is one of the best ways to enjoy the flavour of mushrooms. Serve them on individual plates accompanied by garlic bread.

MAKES 12

12 large cup mushrooms, about 350 g (12 oz) total weight

75 g (3 oz) butter

4 celery sticks, cleaned and finely chopped

1 small onion, skinned and finely chopped

50 g (2 oz) walnuts, finely chopped

75 g (3 oz) fresh breadcrumbs

60 ml (4 tbsp) chopped fresh parsley

30 ml (2 tbsp) lemon juice

salt and freshly ground pepper

1 egg, beaten

50 g (2 oz) Cheddar cheese, grated

90 ml (6 tbsp) chicken stock

1. Wipe the mushrooms and pull out the stalks. Chop the stalks finely.

2. Heat the butter in a medium frying pan and lightly brown the rounded sides of the mushroom caps, a few at a time. Remove from the pan.

3. Add the chopped mushroom stalks, celery, onion and walnuts to the pan and fry quickly for 2–3 minutes, stirring occasionally.

4. Remove from the heat and stir in the breadcrumbs, parsley, lemon juice and seasoning. Bind with the beaten egg.

5. Spoon into the mushroom caps and place side by side in a shallow ovenproof dish which they just fit. Sprinkle a little cheese over each mushroom and pour the stock around the edges of the dish. Bake in the oven at 180°C (350°F) mark 4 for 20–25 minutes. Serve hot.

Warm Mange-tout Timbales

All the mange-tout can be prepared for cooking, and the mange-tout and egg yolk purée completed, several hours in advance—in the morning for dinner that night. The mange-tout timbales can be kept warm for up to 30 minutes before being turned out.

SERVES 6

450 g (1 lb) mange-tout, topped, tailed and cut lengthways into strips

2 eggs, separated

salt and white pepper

225 ml (8 fl oz) whipping cream, whipped

1. Reserve about a quarter of the mange-tout. Cook the remainder in boiling salted water for about 6 minutes or until tender.

2. Drain well, then purée in a blender or food processor with the egg yolks. Pour into a bowl. Add seasoning and fold in the cream.

3. Whisk the egg whites until stiff but not dry, then fold into the mange-tout cream.

4. Divide the mixture between six buttered dariole moulds. Place the moulds in a roasting tin and surround with boiling water. Bake at 180°C (350°F) mark 4 for about 15 minutes or until risen and lightly set.

5. Meanwhile, cook the reserved mange-tout in boiling salted water for 2–3 minutes or until tender but still crisp. Drain well and keep hot.

6. Leave the mange-tout timbales to stand for about 2–3 minutes before turning out on to warmed plates. Arrange the reserved mange-tout around each timbale and serve.

Above: Asparagus with coriander hollandaise sauce (page 20)
Right: Lymeswold with redcurrant jelly (page 20)

Oyster and *W*atercress *T*arts

The watercress purée can be made the day before and kept in a cool place. The oysters can be removed from their shells, and the shells lined with filo pastry in advance, but keep the pastry tightly covered to prevent it drying out.

SERVES 6

350 g (12 oz) young watercress, thick stalks removed
lemon juice
175 ml (6 fl oz) double cream or crème fraîche
18 native oysters
about 50 g (2 oz) unsalted butter, melted
3 sheets of filo pastry

1. Cook the watercress in a little boiling salted water, to which a squeeze of lemon juice has been added, for 2–3 minutes. Drain well.

2. Purée the watercress in a blender or food processor with the cream, then transfer to a small heavy-based saucepan.

3. Open the oyster shells and carefully remove the oysters. Brush the deep shells with melted butter and arrange on one or two baking sheets.

4. Stack the sheets of filo pastry, brushing between them with melted butter. Cut the stack into eighteen 6.5–7.5 cm (2½–3 inch) squares.

5. Line each oyster shell with a square of pastry and brush the top with melted butter. Bake at 200°C (400°F) mark 6 for 5–8 minutes.

6. Meanwhile, gently warm the watercress purée. Add a squeeze of lemon juice to the remaining melted butter.

7. Divide the watercress purée between the filo shells. Place the raw oysters on top and brush with lemon butter. Serve three per person.

*S*teak *T*artare

Guests should help themselves to a portion of steak tartare, some vegetables, herbs and mustard mayonnaise, then mix everything together on their plates with a fork.

SERVES 10

900 g (2 lb) fillet steak
15 ml (1 tbsp) Worcestershire sauce
sea salt
freshly ground black pepper
2 red peppers, cored, seeded and finely diced
2 green peppers, cored, seeded and finely diced
1 Spanish onion, skinned and finely chopped
3 cooked beetroots, skinned and finely diced
75 ml (5 tbsp) capers, chopped
75 ml (5 tbsp) finely chopped fresh parsley
5 egg yolks
30–45 ml (2–3 tbsp) French mustard
450 ml (¾ pint) thick homemade mayonnaise
Tabasco sauce, to taste

1. Trim any fat and membrane off the steak, then put the meat through the fine blade of a mincer or food processor. Turn into a bowl and add the Worcestershire sauce and salt and pepper to taste.

2. Divide the mixture into 10 equal portions. Form into rounds and make a slight hollow in the centre of each one.

3. Arrange the steak patties on a large platter or tray and surround with small mounds of the diced and chopped vegetables and herbs.

4. Beat the egg yolks together, then spoon a little into the hollow in each steak.

5. Beat the mustard into the mayonnaise, add Tabasco and salt and pepper to taste, then transfer to a bowl.

Gravad Lax

Ask your fishmonger for the tail end of a whole salmon; he will most likely charge you less per kg (lb) than for the thick centre fillet. Salmon trout, which is less expensive than salmon, can also be used, if liked.

SERVES 10

15 ml (1 tbsp) caster sugar

15 ml (1 tbsp) salt

15 ml (1 tbsp) black peppercorns, coarsely crushed

60–90 ml (4–6 tbsp) chopped fresh dill or 15–30 ml (1–2 tbsp) dried dillweed

about 700 g (1½ lb) fresh salmon, filleted into 2 pieces

lemon slices, to garnish

FOR THE MUSTARD AND DILL SAUCE

1 egg yolk

30 ml (2 tbsp) German mustard

2.5 ml (½ tsp) sugar

salt and freshly ground black pepper

150 ml (¼ pint) olive oil

30 ml (2 tbsp) red wine vinegar

10 ml (2 tsp) chopped fresh dill or 5 ml (1 tsp) dried dillweed

1. Mix the sugar, salt, peppercorns and dill together in a bowl. Sprinkle a quarter of this mixture in a shallow (non-metal) dish.

2. Put one fillet of the salmon, skin side down, in the dish. Sprinkle over half the remaining mixture, then place the second salmon fillet on top, skin side uppermost. Sprinkle with the remaining mixture and rub it well into the salmon skin.

3. Cover the salmon with foil and place heavy weights on top. Refrigerate for 2–5 days, turning the salmon once every day and basting with the brine that collects in the bottom of the dish.

4. To make the mustard and dill sauce, put the egg yolk, mustard, sugar and salt and pepper to taste in a bowl. Whisk to combine, then add the oil, a drop at a time, whisking until the mixture thickens, as when making mayonnaise.

5. Continue adding the oil very slowly, then, when it has all been incorporated, add the vinegar and dill. (Alternatively, use the dill to garnish the fish.) Taste and adjust the seasoning, then turn into a sauceboat, bowl or jug.

6. To serve, scrape the spice mixture off the salmon with a sharp knife. Remove the skin by gripping the tail end with fingers dipped in salt and working the knife away from you between the skin and the flesh in a sawing action.

7. Cut the flesh into 5 mm (¼ inch) thick slices across the width of the salmon. Arrange on a plate with lemon slices to garnish.

Cod's Roe Ramekins

Smoked cod's roe has a delicious flavour and a little of it goes a long way. These light, airy soufflés are very quickly cooked, so do be ready to serve them immediately.

SERVES 6

225 g (8 oz) smoked cod's roe, skinned

50 g (2 oz) fresh breadcrumbs

15 ml (1 tbsp) chopped fresh parsley

30 ml (2 tbsp) lemon juice

1 egg, separated

150 ml (¼ pint) natural yogurt

pinch of ground mace

salt and freshly ground pepper

1. Put the roe in a blender or food processor. Add the breadcrumbs, parsley, lemon juice, egg yolk, yogurt and mace, season to taste and work together until smooth. Turn into a bowl.

2. Whisk the egg white until stiff, then fold into the mixture.

3. Spoon into six greased ramekin dishes. Bake at 200°C (400°F) mark 6 for 15–20 minutes or until well risen and golden brown. Serve at once, accompanied by fingers of toast.

Mediterranean Prawns with Concassée Tomatoes

The tomatoes can be skinned, seeded and diced the day before. Keep them in the refrigerator, in a covered container.

SERVES 6

1 shallot, skinned and finely chopped

100 ml (4 fl oz) medium dry white wine

125 g (4½ oz) unsalted butter

18 raw Mediterranean prawns, or Dublin Bay prawns (scampi), in their shells

25 ml (1½ tbsp) lemon juice

sea salt

cayenne pepper

2 large tomatoes, skinned, seeded and diced

fresh chives, to garnish

1. Put the shallot and wine in a small saucepan and simmer gently until most of the liquid has evaporated. Melt 40 g (1½ oz) of the butter.

2. Meanwhile, toss the prawns in the lemon juice, seasoned with sea salt and cayenne pepper. Brush with the melted butter and grill for 2–3 minutes, turning frequently.

3. Gently warm the tomatoes in a small saucepan until their juices are reduced.

4. Dice the remaining butter and whisk gradually into the wine mixture, making sure each piece is completely incorporated before adding the next. Season with salt and a pinch of cayenne pepper.

5. Divide the butter sauce between six warmed plates. Remove the tomatoes from the saucepan with a slotted spoon, allowing any excess moisture to drain, and place in the sauce. Place the prawns to the side. Sprinkle a few chives over the sauce and serve.

Smoked Salmon Mousses

Scottish salmon is thought by many to have the best flavour of all. This mousse tastes just as good if made from cheap end cuts or flakes of smoked salmon which can be bought in the required quantity.

SERVES 6

300 ml (10 fl oz) single cream

2 bay leaves

100 g (4 oz) smoked salmon

15 ml (1 tbsp) lemon juice

large pinch of paprika

about 150 ml (¼ pint) milk

15 ml (3 tsp) powdered gelatine

cucumber slices, to garnish

1. Gently heat the cream and bay leaves together in a small saucepan. When warm, remove from the heat and leave to infuse for 2–3 hours.

2. Discard the bay leaves. Pour the cream into a blender or food processor, add the salmon (reserving one small slice to garnish), the lemon juice and paprika and blend together.

3. Transfer to a measuring jug and add enough milk to make up the quantity to 600 ml (1 pint). Stir well together.

4. Sprinkle the gelatine over 45 ml (3 tbsp) water in a small bowl and leave to soak for a few minutes. Place the bowl over a saucepan of simmering water and stir until dissolved. Leave to cool slightly, then whisk into the salmon mixture.

5. Pour the mixture into six ramekin dishes and leave to chill for at least 2 hours. Serve garnished with a small piece of the reserved salmon and cucumber slices.

Right: Mediterranean prawns with concassé tomatoes (above)

Artichoke Hearts in Olive Oil

This starter may be prepared several hours in advance. Keep in a cool place until ready to serve.

SERVES 8

90 ml (6 tbsp) lemon juice
8 globe artichokes
90 ml (6 tbsp) olive oil
2 garlic cloves, skinned
salt and freshly ground pepper

1. Add 30 ml (2 tbsp) of the lemon juice to a large bowl of cold water.

2. Remove the stems and outer leaves from the artichokes. Using a sharp stainless steel knife, slice off the remaining leaves to within 1 cm ($\frac{1}{2}$ inch) of the heart. Remove the chokes with a teaspoon.

3. As the artichoke hearts are prepared, plunge them quickly into the acidulated water, covering them completely. This will prevent them discolouring.

4. Place 450 ml ($\frac{3}{4}$ pint) water in a saucepan with the remaining lemon juice, the olive oil, whole garlic cloves and seasoning. Bring to the boil, then add the artichoke hearts and simmer for 20–25 minutes or until tender.

5. Remove the artichoke hearts with a slotted spoon. Boil the cooking liquid until reduced by half, then strain a little over the artichoke hearts. Leave to cool, then cut the hearts into quarters.

Chicken Liver Pâté

To prevent this pâté drying out while chilling, cover the surface with melted butter. Serve with Melba toast or crusty French bread.

SERVES 8

450 g (1 lb) chicken livers
50 g (2 oz) butter
1 medium onion, skinned and chopped
1 garlic clove, skinned and crushed
75 ml (5 tbsp) double cream
15 ml (1 tbsp) tomato purée
15 ml (1 tbsp) brandy
salt and freshly ground pepper
parsley sprigs, to garnish

1. Clean the chicken livers and dry with absorbent kitchen paper.

2. Heat the butter in a saucepan, add the onion and garlic and cook for about 5 minutes or until the onion is soft. Add the chicken livers and cook for a further 5 minutes. Leave to cool.

3. Add the cream, tomato purée and brandy to the liver mixture and season well.

4. Purée the mixture in a blender or food processor and put into a serving dish. Chill in the refrigerator before serving garnished with fresh parsley sprigs.

FISH AND SEAFOOD

Grey Mullet Cooked in Lemon and Red Wine

If you can find it when in season, grey mullet is a real delicacy. Otherwise, use wild or farmed trout. Cox's apples give a distinctive flavour but another eating apple could be substituted.

SERVES 4

15 g (½ oz) butter
450 g (1 lb) Cox's apples, peeled, cored and sliced
6 spring onions, sliced
finely grated rind and juice of 1 lemon
1–2 garlic cloves, skinned and crushed
salt and freshly ground pepper
4 grey mullet, each weighing about 275 g (10 oz)
2 lemons, sliced
300 ml (½ pint) dry red wine
60 ml (4 tbsp) double cream

1. To make the stuffing, melt the butter in a medium saucepan and lightly fry the apples, spring onions, lemon rind, 30 ml (2 tbsp) of the lemon juice and the garlic. Season to taste.
2. Make three slashes across both sides of each grey mullet and insert the lemon slices. Sprinkle the cavity of each fish with the remaining lemon juice and fill with the stuffing. Put into a large ovenproof dish.
3. Pour over the red wine and bake at 180°C (350°F) mark 4 for 20–30 minutes or until the fish is tender.
4. Remove the fish from the dish and place on a warmed serving dish. Keep hot.
5. Pour the cooking liquid into a small saucepan, stir in the cream and reheat gently. Pour over the fish and serve.

Salmon with Fennel Sauce

Fennel has an interesting, aniseed-like flavour that complements the flavour of salmon perfectly.

SERVES 4

4 salmon steaks, each weighing about 175 g (6 oz)
2 shallots, skinned and chopped
1 small fennel bulb, finely chopped
1 bay leaf
2 fresh parsley stalks, crushed
150 ml (¼ pint) dry white wine
2 egg yolks
100 g (4 oz) butter, softened
salt and freshly ground pepper
lemon juice, to taste
fresh fennel sprigs, to garnish

1. Place the salmon steaks in a shallow ovenproof dish. Scatter the shallots, fennel, bay leaf and parsley over the top. Pour in the wine, cover tightly and bake at 180°C (350°F) mark 4 for 15 minutes or until the fish is tender.
2. Strain off 100 ml (4 fl oz) of the cooking liquor. Re-cover the salmon and keep warm.
3. Boil the strained liquor until reduced to 15 ml (1 tbsp). Beat the egg yolks together in a medium heatproof bowl, then stir in the reduced liquor and work in half of the butter.
4. Place the bowl over a saucepan of simmering water and whisk with a balloon whisk until the butter has melted. Gradually whisk in the remaining butter. Remove from the heat.
5. Remove 10 ml (2 tsp) of the cooked fennel from the salmon dish and add to the sauce. Season to taste, adding a little lemon juice. Transfer the salmon to a warmed plate. Spoon the sauce over and garnish with fennel.

Salmon with Herb Sauce

The pink flesh and delicate flavour of salmon is admirably complemented by the pretty green sauce. If you can't get the herbs specified, use others, but beware of those with an overpowering flavour.

SERVES 4

900 g (2 lb) salmon, cleaned

45 ml (3 tbsp) lemon juice

50 g (2 oz) butter

salt and freshly ground pepper

1 bunch of watercress, trimmed and roughly chopped

100 g (4 oz) fresh spinach leaves, roughly chopped

45 ml (3 tbsp) chopped fresh parsley

30 ml (2 tbsp) chopped fresh chervil

5 ml (1 tsp) chopped fresh dill

150 ml ($\frac{1}{4}$ pint) mayonnaise

fresh herbs and whole unpeeled cooked prawns, to garnish (optional)

1. Place the fish in the centre of a large piece of foil. Add 30 ml (2 tbsp) of the lemon juice, then dot with 25 g (1 oz) of the butter. Season to taste.

2. Seal the foil, weigh the fish and place on a baking sheet. Calculate the cooking time at 10 minutes per 450 g (1 lb). Bake at 180°C (350°F) mark 4 until tender.

3. Remove the fish from the foil, reserving the cooking liquor, then carefully remove the skin while still warm. Arrange the fish on a serving dish and leave to cool.

4. To make the sauce, put the cooking liquor and the remaining 25 g (1 oz) butter in a saucepan and heat gently. Add the watercress, spinach, parsley, chervil and dill, then cook for 2–3 minutes or until softened.

5. Put the sauce in a blender or food processor and blend until smooth. Transfer to a bowl, add the remaining lemon juice and season to taste. Leave to cool, then fold in the mayonnaise. Turn into a small serving jug and refrigerate until required.

6. When the fish is cold, garnish with fresh herbs and whole prawns, if liked. Serve with the herb sauce.

Red Mullet Baked in Paper

Red mullet is known as the woodcock of the sea because you can eat it all—there's no need to remove the insides. Cooking in paper conserves all the juices, and the parcels, when opened at table, show the attractive red colour to advantage.

SERVES 4

4 red mullet, each weighing about 225 g (8 oz)

30 ml (2 tbsp) chopped fresh parsley

1 onion, skinned and sliced

100 g (4 oz) mushrooms, chopped

finely grated rind and juice of 2 lemons

salt and freshly ground pepper

1. Cut four squares of greaseproof paper, each large enough to wrap one of the fish. Place the fish on top, then divide the remaining ingredients between them. Fold the paper to make secure parcels.

2. Place the parcels on a baking sheet and bake at 180°C (350°F) mark 4 for 30 minutes or until the fish is tender. Serve the fish in their parcels.

Right: Salmon with herb sauce (above)

Sole with Mussels in Tarragon Cream Sauce

Seafood lovers will delight in this special combination of sole and mussels.

SERVES 4

1.2 litres (2 pints) mussels in their shells

100 ml (4 fl oz) dry white wine

1 shallot, skinned and finely chopped

sprig of fresh thyme

3 parsley sprigs

salt and white pepper

4 sole fillets, skinned

5 ml (1 tsp) finely chopped tarragon

150 ml ($\frac{1}{4}$ pint) double cream

small tarragon sprigs and lemon slices, to garnish

1. Scrub the mussels under cold running water and discard any that do not close when sharply tapped. Remove the beards.

2. Put 60 ml (4 tbsp) of the wine in a saucepan with the shallot, thyme and parsley, and bring to the boil. Add the mussels, cover and cook over a high heat for 4–5 minutes, shaking often.

3. Remove the mussels from their shells, discarding any that have not opened. Strain the juice from the mussels with the cooking liquid and return to the rinsed-out pan.

4. Season the sole fillets, lay them in the liquid and poach gently for 4–5 minutes or until the flesh is just opaque. Transfer the sole to a plate, add the mussels, cover and keep hot.

5. Stir the remaining wine into the cooking liquid with half the tarragon. Boil until reduced to about 30 ml (2 tbsp). Stir in the cream and simmer until thickened. Add the remaining tarragon, reheat gently and season. Coat four warmed serving plates with the sauce.

6. Carefully place the sole on the sauce. Place some of the mussels along the length of the sole and arrange the remainder around the side. Garnish with tarragon and lemon.

Mousseline of Sole with Prawns

This elegant fish main course is cooked in individual ramekin dishes which are then turned out on to one dish and coated in a deliciously rich sauce.

SERVES 6

450 g (1 lb) sole fillets, skinned and chopped

50 g (2 oz) peeled prawns

1 egg white

1.25 ml ($\frac{1}{4}$ tsp) salt

1.25 ml ($\frac{1}{4}$ tsp) white pepper

450 ml ($\frac{3}{4}$ pint) double cream

3 egg yolks, beaten

75 g (3 oz) butter, softened

10 ml (2 tsp) lemon juice

5 ml (1 tsp) tomato purée

fresh dill sprigs and whole prawns in their shells, to garnish

1. Combine the chopped fish with the prawns, egg white and seasoning. Put the mixture in a blender or food processor with 300 ml ($\frac{1}{2}$ pint) cream and blend until smooth.

2. Butter six 150 ml ($\frac{1}{4}$ pint) ovenproof ramekin dishes and press the mixture well down into the dishes. Chill, covered, for 3 hours.

3. Place the ramekins in a roasting tin and pour in enough boiling water to come halfway up the dishes. Cook in the oven at 150°C (300°F) mark 2 for 30–40 minutes. Turn out on to a wire rack to drain. Keep warm.

4. Put the egg yolks, a knob of butter and the lemon juice in the top of a double boiler or in a heatproof bowl over a pan of simmering water. Stir until of a coating consistency.

5. Remove from the heat and slowly beat in the remaining butter and the tomato purée. Whip the remaining cream until softly stiff and fold into the sauce. Return to the heat to thicken without boiling.

6. Place the moulds in a warmed serving dish and coat with the sauce. Garnish with dill and whole prawns and serve hot.

Hot Fish Loaf

Hake, a cousin of cod, is available all year round. It has a good, flaky texture and is ideally suited to this recipe, where the flavour is sparked up with prawns, garlic and anchovy essence to make a tasty loaf, served with a cheese sauce.

SERVES 6

---

65 g (2½ oz) butter

1 garlic clove, skinned and crushed

75 ml (5 tbsp) plain flour

750 ml (1¼ pints) milk

550 g (1¼ lb) hake fillets, skinned and chopped

150 ml (¼ pint) whipping cream

10 ml (2 tsp) anchovy essence

3 eggs

1 egg yolk

salt and freshly ground pepper

30 ml (2 tbsp) chopped fresh parsley

100 g (4 oz) peeled prawns, chopped

50 g (2 oz) mature Cheddar cheese, grated

watercress sprigs and 6 whole cooked prawns in their shells, to garnish

---

1. Lightly butter and base-line a 1.6 litre (2¾ pint) loaf tin or terrine.

2. Melt 40 g (1½ oz) of the butter in a saucepan. Add the garlic. Stir in 45 ml (3 tbsp) of the flour and cook gently, stirring, for 2 minutes. Remove from the heat and gradually stir in 450 ml (¾ pint) of the milk. Bring to the boil, stirring constantly, then simmer for 2 minutes until thick and smooth.

3. Transfer the sauce to a blender or food processor and add the raw chopped fish, cream, anchovy essence, eggs and yolk. Blend to a purée, then season lightly.

4. Spoon half the fish mixture into the tin and sprinkle with parsley and half the prawns. Spoon in the rest of the fish mixture. Cover tightly with buttered greaseproof paper.

5. Place in a roasting tin and pour in enough hot water to come halfway up the sides of the loaf tin. Cook in the oven at 150°C (300°F) mark 2 for about 1¾ hours.

6. Just before the fish loaf is cooked, make the sauce. Put the remaining 25 g (1 oz) butter, 30 ml (2 tbsp) flour and remaining milk in a saucepan. Heat, whisking continuously, until the sauce thickens, boils and is smooth. Simmer for 1–2 minutes. Stir in the grated cheese and remaining prawns. Season to taste.

7. Invert the loaf on to a warm serving dish and tilt slightly to drain off juice. Remove cooking container. Spoon a little sauce over the loaf and garnish with watercress and prawns. Serve the remaining sauce separately.

Skate with Capers

Skate has a soft, pinkish tinge. The wings may look bony but in fact the bones are soft and gelatinous, and the flesh is easily picked off them when the fish is cooked. The delicacy of the flavour is perfectly complemented by the sharp piquancy of capers.

SERVES 4

---

2 skate wings, each weighing about 550 g (1¼ lb), halved

50 g (2 oz) butter

45 ml (3 tbsp) drained capers

30 ml (2 tbsp) vinegar from the capers

---

1. Put the skate in a roasting tin and cover with salted water. Bring to the boil, then simmer for 10–15 minutes or until tender.

2. Meanwhile, melt the butter in a small saucepan and cook until it turns golden brown. Add the capers and vinegar and cook until bubbling.

3. Drain the fish and place on serving plates. Pour over the sauce and serve at once accompanied by new potatoes.

Above: Mousseline of sole with prawns (page 32)
Right: Skate with capers (page 33)

Langoustine Thermidor with Rice Pilaf

If using cooked langoustines (scampi), remove the meat from the shells and use 300 ml (½ pint) fish stock made with the langoustine shells, then strained.

SERVES 4

750 ml (1¼ pints) dry white wine

1 large onion, skinned and sliced

1 medium carrot, sliced

1 celery stick, sliced

6 parsley sprigs

1 bay leaf

6 peppercorns

1.25 ml (¼ tsp) chopped fresh thyme

15 ml (1 tbsp) chopped fresh tarragon

1.8 kg (4 lb) medium langoustines (about 36–40), preferably alive

75 g (3 oz) butter

175 g (6 oz) button mushrooms, sliced

20 ml (4 tsp) lemon juice

60 ml (4 tbsp) brandy

15 ml (1 tbsp) plain flour

2.5 ml (½ tsp) mustard powder

150 ml (¼ pint) double cream

2 egg yolks

pinch of cayenne pepper

salt and freshly ground pepper

25 g (1 oz) freshly grated Parmesan cheese

FOR THE RICE PILAF

30 ml (2 tbsp) olive oil

1 medium onion, skinned and chopped

225 g (8 oz) long grain rice

500 ml (18 fl oz) fish stock

salt and freshly ground pepper

15 ml (1 tbsp) chopped fresh parsley

1. Place the wine, onion, carrot, celery, parsley, bay leaf, peppercorns, thyme and tarragon in a very large saucepan with 900 ml (1½ pints) water. Cover and simmer gently for 15 minutes.

2. Return the mixture to the boil and add about a quarter of the langoustines. They must be completely immersed in liquid, so do not add too many at one time. Bring back to the boil, then simmer for 2 minutes. Remove the langoustines from the pan using a slotted spoon.

3. Repeat this process until all the langoustines are cooked. Allow to cool, then remove the shells. To do this, separate the head from the body and, using scissors, cut down the underside of the body. The tail meat can easily be removed. Reserve a few langoustine heads for garnish, if wished.

4. Strain the cooking liquid, then boil rapidly until reduced to 300 ml (½ pint).

5. Meanwhile, make the rice pilaf. Heat the oil in a saucepan and fry the onion for about 5 minutes or until soft. Stir in the rice and fry until transparent. Add the stock, bring to the boil, cover and simmer for 15–20 minutes or until the stock has been absorbed. Taste and adjust the seasoning, stir in the chopped parsley and keep hot.

6. Melt 25 g (1 oz) of the butter in a small saucepan and fry the mushrooms for 3 minutes. Add the lemon juice and set aside.

7. Melt 25 g (1 oz) of the remaining butter and fry the langoustine meat for 1 minute. Pour over the brandy and boil until reduced to 15 ml (1 tbsp).

8. Melt the remaining butter and stir in the flour and mustard. Cook, stirring, for 1 minute. Remove from the heat and gradually stir in the reduced stock. Bring to the boil, stirring, then simmer for 5 minutes.

9. Mix the cream and egg yolks together and stir into the sauce over gentle heat. Cook, stirring, until thickened slightly.

10. Stir in the mushrooms and their juices, and the langoustines with their juices. Stir in the cayenne and adjust the seasoning. Transfer the mixture to a flameproof dish, sprinkle with the cheese and cook under a hot grill until golden. Garnish with langoustine heads, if liked, and serve at once with the rice pilaf.

Platter of Fish and Shellfish

You can use whatever fish you like, or what is available to you where you live, but try to provide a variety of different types. Firm-fleshed white fish is better than softer fish such as sole or plaice.

SERVES 8

8 pieces skinned turbot fillet, each weighing about 50 g (2 oz)

8 pieces skinned sea bass fillet, each weighing about 50 g (2 oz)

claw and tail meat from 4 freshly cooked lobsters, each weighing about 600 g (1¼ lb)

8 pieces skinned John Dory fillet, each weighing about 75 g (3 oz)

8 scallops

fresh chervil, lemon balm sprigs and peeled lime segments, to garnish

FOR THE STEAMING LIQUOR

1 shallot, skinned and finely chopped

175 ml (6 fl oz) medium-bodied dry white wine

100 ml (4 fl oz) fish stock

2 fresh lemon balm sprigs

3 large fresh chervil sprigs

1 bay leaf, broken

salt and freshly ground pepper

FOR THE SAUCE

45 ml (3 tbsp) olive oil

2 lobster shells, crushed and pounded

3 shallots, skinned and finely chopped

2 young carrots, finely chopped

50 ml (2 fl oz) whisky

5 fresh parsley sprigs

10 green peppercorns

2 bay leaves, broken

450 ml (¾ pint) fish stock

300 ml (½ pint) medium-bodied dry white wine

225 g (8 oz) unsalted butter, diced

salt and white pepper

1. To make the sauce, heat the oil in a saucepan, add the lobster shells and cook, stirring occasionally, for 5 minutes.

2. Stir in the shallots and carrots, and cook gently, stirring occasionally, until the shallots are softened.

3. Stir in the whisky and set alight. When the flames have died down, stir in the parsley, peppercorns, bay leaves, stock and wine. Cover and simmer for 20–25 minutes.

4. Strain the liquid into a measuring jug, pressing down well on the vegetables to extract as much liquid from them as possible. There should be about 350 ml (12 fl oz). If insufficiently reduced, boil down further. Set aside.

5. Put the ingredients for the steaming liquor into the bottom of a steamer or large saucepan and bring to the boil. Place the turbot in the steaming basket, place over the liquor and cover. Steam for 30 seconds.

6. Add the sea bass and steam for 1 minute, then add the lobster and John Dory and steam for 2 minutes longer. Add the scallops and their corals and steam for a final 30 seconds. Remove from the heat but keep covered.

7. Over a very low heat, gradually whisk the butter into the sauce liquid, making sure each piece is fully incorporated before adding the next. Season and keep warm over a very low heat. Do not allow to boil.

8. Arrange the fish and shellfish on a large warmed platter and garnish with sprigs of chervil and lemon balm and lime segments. Serve with the sauce in a warmed sauceboat.

Overleaf: Artichoke hearts in olive oil (page 28), geranium cream with red summer fruits (page 88), platter of fish and shellfish (above)

Tagliatelle with Seafood and Champagne Sauce

A scrumptious sauce transforms fresh pasta into a special occasion dish.
SERVES 4

16 fresh mussels, scrubbed and beards removed

175 g (6 oz) fresh clams, scrubbed

150 ml (¼ pint) fish stock

1 red mullet, weighing about 300 g (11 oz), filleted

175 g (6 oz) salmon fillet, skinned

4 large uncooked Pacific prawns, peeled

4 fresh scallops

225 g (8 oz) fresh tagliatelle

75 g (3 oz) butter

salt and freshly ground pepper

50 g (2 oz) leek, cut in fine julienne strips

150 ml (¼ pint) champagne or dry sparkling white wine

300 ml (½ pint) double cream

pinch of cayenne pepper

12 fresh basil leaves

1. Discard any open mussels or clams which do not close when tapped. Place in a pan with the stock, cover and cook over high heat for several minutes or until the shells open. Discard any closed shells. Leave to cool in the stock, then remove the mussels and clams from their shells. Strain the stock through muslin and reserve.

2. Cut the fish fillets into 1 cm (½ inch) strips. Remove the vein from each prawn and cut in half. Separate the coral from each scallop and cut the scallops in half crossways.

3. Cook the tagliatelle in boiling salted water with a dash of oil for 2–3 minutes or until *al dente*. Drain and toss in half the butter. Season.

4. Melt the remaining butter and fry the leeks, prawns and scallop coral for 30 seconds. Add the fish fillets, champagne and reserved stock, and simmer for 1 minute. Carefully remove all the fish from the pan and keep warm.

5. Boil the liquid rapidly until reduced by half. Add the cream and boil rapidly until reduced and thickened. Taste and adjust the seasoning and add the cayenne pepper.

6. Return the fish to the sauce with the mussels, clams, scallops and basil. Warm through gently and serve at once with the tagliatelle.

Fish Wellington

This fish version of the classic beef dish is very easy to prepare and makes an unusual lunch party dish.
SERVES 6–8

100 g (4 oz) mushrooms, wiped and chopped

50 g (2 oz) onion, skinned and finely chopped

25 g (1 oz) butter

175 g (6 oz) smooth liver pâté, or liver sausage

60 ml (4 tbsp) double cream

salt and freshly ground pepper

2 large fillets of cod or haddock, about 900 g (2 lb) total weight, skinned

368 g (13 oz) packet frozen puff pastry, thawed

beaten egg, to glaze

1. Fry the chopped mushrooms and onion in the butter for about 5 minutes or until soft.

2. Mash the liver pâté or sausage in a bowl and stir in the cream, onion and mushrooms. Season.

3. On a lightly floured surface, roll out the pastry to a rectangle measuring 35 × 30 cm (14 × 12 inches). Place one fish fillet in the centre of the pastry and spread filling mixture over it. Top with the other fillet. Trim the pastry round, allowing a good 10 cm (4 inch) border.

4. Brush round the edges of the pastry with beaten egg, then carefully fold it over the fish and neatly wrap it up like a parcel. Place on a baking sheet with the sealed edges down. Brush with beaten egg. Roll and cut the pastry trimmings into fish shapes and place on top.

5. Bake in the oven at 220°C (425°F) mark 7 for about 25 minutes or until the pastry is golden brown and the fish is cooked through.

Meat Main Courses

Beef in Wine with Walnuts

Ground walnuts add an interesting texture to this tasty casserole. Buy walnut pieces, which are cheaper than halves.

SERVES 6

900 g (2 lb) shin of beef, trimmed and cut into 2.5 cm (1 inch) cubes

150 ml ($\frac{1}{4}$ pint) dry red wine

15 ml (1 tbsp) vegetable oil

15 g ($\frac{1}{2}$ oz) butter

1 small onion, skinned and finely chopped

1 garlic clove, skinned and crushed

5 ml (1 tsp) ground allspice

30 ml (2 tbsp) plain flour

150 ml ($\frac{1}{4}$ pint) beef stock

50 g (2 oz) shelled walnut pieces, ground

3 medium parsnips, peeled and cut into 5 cm (2 inch) lengths, about 1 cm ($\frac{1}{2}$ inch) wide

salt and freshly ground pepper

chopped walnuts, to garnish

1. Put the beef in a bowl with the wine and mix well. Cover and leave to marinate overnight, stirring occasionally.

2. Drain the meat from the marinade, reserving the marinade. Heat the oil and butter in a large frying pan, add the beef, a few pieces at a time, and brown quickly. Remove from the pan with a slotted spoon and put in an ovenproof casserole.

3. Add the onion and garlic to the frying pan and fry until beginning to brown. Stir in the allspice, flour, reserved marinade, stock and walnuts. Bring to the boil, stirring constantly.

4. Pour into the casserole and add the parsnips. Season lightly to taste. Cover and cook at 170°C

(325°F) mark 3 for 2$\frac{1}{2}$–3 hours or until tender.

5. Serve hot, straight from the casserole, sprinkled with the chopped walnuts.

Beef in Stout

This is a simple dish packed with goodness. Stout makes a delicious gravy in a casserole.

SERVES 4–6

15 g ($\frac{1}{2}$ oz) butter

about 15 ml (1 tbsp) vegetable oil

900 g (2 lb) stewing steak, cut into 5 cm (2 inch) cubes

4 medium onions, skinned and sliced

225 g (8 oz) button mushrooms, halved

salt and freshly ground pepper

30 ml (2 tbsp) plain flour

300 ml ($\frac{1}{2}$ pint) stout

1 bay leaf

5 ml (1 tsp) dark soft brown sugar

1. Heat the butter and oil in a large flameproof casserole and cook the meat for 10 minutes or until browned all over. Remove the meat from the pan with a slotted spoon.

2. Add the onions and mushrooms to the pan, adding more oil if necessary, and fry until softened. Season to taste, add the flour and stir well so that the flour absorbs the fat.

3. Return the meat to the pan, pour in the stout and add the bay leaf and brown sugar. Stir well.

4. Cover and cook gently, either on top of the cooker or in the oven at 180°C (350°F) mark 4 for about 2$\frac{1}{2}$ hours or until the meat is tender.

Overleaf: Julienned courgettes in garlic butter (page 92), beef pockets stuffed with mushrooms (page 44)

Beef Olives

The actual origin of the name of this very English dish is a little uncertain—it is most likely that it is so called because the shape resembles olives.

SERVES 4

75 g (3 oz) bacon, rinded and chopped

1 small onion, skinned and chopped

10 ml (2 tsp) finely chopped fresh parsley

100 g (4 oz) fresh breadcrumbs

50 g (2 oz) shredded suet

1.25 ml ($\frac{1}{4}$ tsp) mixed dried herbs

1 lemon

1 small egg, beaten

salt and freshly ground pepper

about 700 g (1$\frac{1}{2}$ lb) topside of beef, cut into 8 thin slices

about 15 ml (1 tbsp) prepared English mustard

2 bacon rashers, rinded and chopped

2 shallots, skinned and chopped

1 carrot, chopped

1 very small turnip, chopped

300 ml ($\frac{1}{2}$ pint) brown stock, preferably veal

150 ml ($\frac{1}{4}$ pint) red wine

50 ml (2 fl oz) Marsala

1 bay leaf

parsley sprigs, to garnish

cooked baby carrots, baby turnips and whole shallots, to serve

1. Mix the first six ingredients together, add the grated rind of half the lemon and 5 ml (1 tsp) of the juice. Bind with the egg, then season.
2. Flatten each slice of beef between two sheets of damp greaseproof paper, then spread sparingly with mustard. Divide the stuffing between the slices, fold the sides over and roll up into neat parcels. Secure with fine string.
3. Heat the chopped bacon rashers gently in a shallow flameproof casserole until the fat runs, then remove the bacon with a slotted spoon.
4. Place the rolls in the casserole and fry until browned. Remove with a slotted spoon.
5. Add the shallots, carrot and turnip and fry until the shallots are soft. Stir in the stock, wine and Marsala, and bring to the boil.

6. Return the bacon and beef rolls to the casserole, add the bay leaf and season lightly. Cover with foil and the lid and cook at 170°C (325°F) mark 3 for about 1$\frac{1}{2}$ hours.
7. Transfer the beef rolls to a warmed serving plate. Remove the bay leaf from the liquid and purée the liquid in a blender or food processor. Transfer to a saucepan, bring to the boil and boil for a few minutes to thicken slightly. Taste and adjust the seasoning and pour over the beef.
8. Garnish with parsley sprigs and serve surrounded by carrots, turnips and shallots.

Beef Pockets Stuffed with Mushrooms

Mushrooms make marvellous stuffings and are always available. Ginger wine is an English speciality with a strong positive flavour.

SERVES 4

4 thick-cut steaks, each weighing 175 g (6 oz)

salt and freshly ground pepper

15 g ($\frac{1}{2}$ oz) butter

175 g (6 oz) mushrooms, finely chopped

1 garlic clove, skinned and crushed

1 large onion, skinned and finely chopped

15 ml (1 tbsp) chopped fresh parsley

15 ml (1 tbsp) ginger wine

15 ml (1 tbsp) fresh wholemeal breadcrumbs

15 ml (1 tbsp) double cream

1. Using a sharp, pointed knife, make a horizontal cut in each steak without cutting all the way through. Season to taste.
2. Melt the butter in a medium saucepan and lightly cook the mushrooms, garlic and onion for 5 minutes or until softened. Remove from the heat.
3. Add the parsley, ginger wine, breadcrumbs and cream. Mix together well.
4. Generously fill each steak with stuffing.
5. Grill the steaks for 5–15 minutes or until cooked to taste. Serve at once.

Crown Roast

This is a spectacular dinner party dish. Some supermarkets now stock prepared crown roasts, or ask your butcher in advance to prepare one for you. If you do it yourself, make sure that only the best ends of neck are chined.

SERVES 6

2 best end necks of lamb, each with 6 cutlets, chined

15 g ($\frac{1}{2}$ oz) butter

1 medium onion, skinned and chopped

3 celery sticks, chopped

2 eating apples, cored and chopped

100 g (4 oz) fresh breadcrumbs

30 ml (2 tbsp) chopped fresh mint

grated rind and juice of $\frac{1}{2}$ lemon

1 egg

salt and freshly ground pepper

30 ml (2 tbsp) plain flour

450 ml ($\frac{3}{4}$ pint) lamb or beef stock

mint sprigs, to garnish

1. Trim each cutlet bone to a depth of 2.5 cm (1 inch).

2. Bend the joints round, fat sides inwards, and sew together, using strong cotton or fine string, to form a crown. Cover the exposed bones with foil.

3. Melt the butter in a saucepan and cook the onion, celery and apples until brown. Stir in the breadcrumbs, mint, lemon rind and juice and egg. Season to taste and cool. Fill the centre of the joint with the stuffing and weigh.

4. Place the joint in a small roasting tin. Roast at 180°C (350°F) mark 4 for 25 minutes per 450 g (1 lb) plus 25 minutes. Baste occasionally and cover with foil if necessary.

5. Transfer the roast to a warmed serving dish and keep warm. Drain off all but 30 ml (2 tbsp) of the fat in the roasting tin, then add the flour and blend well. Cook for 2–3 minutes, stirring continuously. Add the stock and boil for 2–3 minutes. Adjust the seasoning and serve hot with the joint. Garnish with sprigs of mint.

Beef Wellington

The Duke of Wellington was a highly prominent statesman and soldier of the nineteenth century. This dish bears his name because the finished joint was thought to resemble one of his brown boots.

SERVES 8

1.4 kg (3 lb) fillet of beef

freshly ground pepper

15 ml (1 tbsp) vegetable oil

40 g (1$\frac{1}{2}$ oz) butter

225 g (8 oz) button mushrooms, sliced

175 g (6 oz) smooth liver pâté

368 g (13 oz) packet frozen puff pastry, thawed

1 egg, beaten, to glaze

1. Trim and tie up the fillet at intervals so it retains its shape. Season to taste with pepper. Heat the oil and 15 g ($\frac{1}{2}$ oz) of the butter in a large frying pan, add the meat and fry briskly on all sides. Press down with a wooden spoon while frying to seal well.

2. Put the meat in a roasting tin and roast at 220°C (425°F) mark 7 for 20 minutes. Set the beef aside to cool, then remove the string.

3. Meanwhile, melt the remaining butter in a saucepan and cook the mushrooms until soft. Leave until cold, then blend with the pâté.

4. On a lightly floured surface, roll out the pastry to a large rectangle about 33 × 28 cm (13 × 11 inches) and 0.5 cm ($\frac{1}{4}$ inch) thick. Trim the pastry to neaten, reserving the trimmings.

5. Spread the pâté mixture down the centre of the pastry and place the meat on top. Brush the edges of the pastry with beaten egg.

6. Fold the long pastry edges over the meat and turn the parcel over so that the join is underneath. Fold the ends under on a baking sheet.

7. Decorate with leaves cut from the pastry trimmings. Brush with the remaining egg and bake at 220°C (425°F) mark 7 for 50–60 minutes, depending on how well done you like your beef. Cover with foil after 25 minutes. Allow to rest for 10 minutes before serving.

Provençal Roast Lamb

Make the herb and garlic paste the day before. If you like, rub it over the lamb the day before, too.
SERVES 6

45 ml (3 tbsp) mixed chopped fresh herbs,
e.g. rosemary, savory, marjoram and thyme

3 garlic cloves, skinned and crushed

salt and freshly ground pepper

60 ml (4 tbsp) olive oil

1.8 kg (4 lb) boned leg of lamb

100 ml (4 fl oz) red wine

25 g (1 oz) butter, cut into 6 pieces

1. Put the herbs in a mortar with the garlic and pound to form a paste. Season and gradually work in the olive oil.

2. Rub this mixture over all the surfaces of the meat, particularly in the cavity. Tie into a neat shape and place in a roasting tin. Leave at room temperature for 2 hours.

3. Roast the lamb at 220°C (425°F) mark 7 for 15 minutes, then reduce the heat to 180°C (350°F) mark 4 and continue roasting for 1 hour 25 minutes. The meat will be pink inside, so if you prefer it well done, roast for 20–25 minutes longer. Baste occasionally with a little of the wine during cooking.

4. Remove the lamb to a warmed serving platter and keep warm while you make the sauce. Pour off most of the fat from the roasting tin. Heat the remaining fat and sediment until it is very hot, then pour in the wine, scraping down the sediment and stirring all the time. Reduce the heat and simmer for 5 minutes, stirring. Swirl the butter into the pan, a piece at a time, to thicken.

5. To serve, slice the meat and pour a little sauce over each slice.

Lamb with Cherries

Juicy red cherries add a slight sharpness to this unusual casserole. Flavours and textures blend deliciously as the ingredients cook in red wine.
SERVES 6

225 g (8 oz) streaky bacon rashers, rinded and chopped

15 g (½ oz) butter

1.4 kg (3 lb) boneless leg or shoulder of lamb, cut into 4 cm (1½ inch) cubes

1 medium onion, skinned and sliced

1 medium carrot, sliced

1 celery stick, sliced

1 garlic clove, skinned and sliced

600 ml (1 pint) dry red wine

bouquet garni

pinch of freshly grated nutmeg

salt and freshly ground pepper

450 g (1 lb) fresh red cherries, stoned

1. In a large frying pan, fry the bacon in its own fat until browned. Add the butter to the pan and fry the lamb, a little at a time, until browned. Remove from the pan with the bacon and put in an ovenproof casserole.

2. Fry the onion, carrot, celery and garlic in the fat remaining in the pan for about 5 minutes or until lightly browned. Add the vegetables to the casserole.

3. Pour over the wine and add the bouquet garni, nutmeg and salt and pepper to taste. Cover and cook at 150°C (300°F) mark 2 for about 2½ hours.

4. Thirty minutes before the end of the cooking time, stir the cherries into the casserole and continue cooking until the meat is tender and the cherries soft.

Right: Lamb with cherries (above)

Leg of Lamb with Crab Meat Stuffing

This is based on an early nineteenth century recipe, the flavours of which combine extremely well without overpowering each other. The dill goes well with both lamb and crab.

SERVES 6

salt and freshly ground pepper

1.8 kg (4 lb) leg of young lamb, boned

225 g (8 oz) crab meat

25 g (1 oz) fresh breadcrumbs

finely grated rind of 1 lemon

freshly grated nutmeg

pinch of cayenne pepper

1 egg yolk

1 celery stick, finely chopped

white part of 1 thin leek, finely chopped

75 ml (3 fl oz) dry white wine

FOR THE SAUCE

225 g (8 oz) unsalted butter, diced

25 g (1 oz) plain flour

about 22.5 ml (1½ tbsp) finely chopped fresh dill

lemon juice, to taste

salt and white pepper

1. Season the lamb inside and out. Mix the crab meat, breadcrumbs, lemon rind, nutmeg, cayenne and seasoning together and bind lightly with egg yolk. Fill the cavity in the leg with the mixture and sew it up.

2. Place the celery and leek in a casserole. Season and place the lamb on top. Pour the wine over, cover and cook at 180°C (350°F) mark 4 for about 1½ hours or until the lamb is almost tender.

3. Transfer the lamb to a rack placed in a roasting tin and return it to the oven for about 20 minutes to brown the outside.

4. Meanwhile, make the sauce. Melt one-third of the butter in a saucepan. Blend the flour with 150 ml (¼ pint) water and whisk into the melted butter, using a balloon whisk. Heat gently until simmering, then cook over a low heat for about 20 minutes, stirring occasionally.

5. Gradually whisk the remaining butter into the sauce, making sure each piece is fully incorporated before adding the next. Add the dill and lemon juice to taste and season with salt and pepper. Cook over a low heat for about 15 minutes.

6. While the sauce is cooking, remove the lamb from the oven and leave in a warm place.

7. Serve the lamb, carved into slices, accompanied by the dill and butter sauce.

Lamb Cutlets Reform

Reform sauce is mouth-wateringly piquant and deliciously seasoned with herbs and spices. It was invented in the 1830s by the great French chef Alexis Soyer. This is a simplified version of the traditional recipe, and omits ingredients such as hard-boiled egg white and cooked tongue which would make the sauce too elaborate for modern tastes.

SERVES 4

15 g (½ oz) butter

1 small onion, skinned and finely chopped

1 medium carrot, finely sliced

50 g (2 oz) lean ham, cut into thin strips

60 ml (4 tbsp) red wine vinegar

45 ml (3 tbsp) port

600 ml (1 pint) lamb or chicken stock

2 cloves

2 blades of mace

1 bay leaf

4 juniper berries, crushed

pinch of dried thyme

8 lamb cutlets, each weighing about 75 g (3 oz)

50 g (2 oz) cooked ham, finely minced

50 g (2 oz) fresh breadcrumbs

1 egg, beaten

15 ml (1 tbsp) cornflour

1. To make the Reform sauce, melt the butter in a medium saucepan, then add the onion, carrot and ham and cook gently until just turning brown. Add the vinegar and port and boil rapidly until almost all the liquid has evaporated.

2. Remove the pan from the heat and add the stock, cloves, mace, bay leaf, juniper berries and thyme. Stir well, return to the heat and bring to the boil. Lower the heat and simmer gently for about 30 minutes.

3. Meanwhile, trim the cutlets to remove most of the surrounding fat. Scrape the bone absolutely clean to within 2.5 cm (1 inch) of the 'eye' of the meat.

4. Mix the minced ham and breadcrumbs together. Brush each cutlet with beaten egg and coat with the ham and breadcrumb mixture. Cover and chill until required.

5. Strain the sauce and return to the pan. Blend the cornflour with about 30 ml (2 tbsp) water and add to the sauce. Stir well and bring the sauce to the boil, stirring continuously. Simmer until thickened.

6. Grill the cutlets for about 4 minutes on each side or until golden brown. Arrange the cutlets on a warmed serving dish and garnish each one with a cutlet frill. Reheat the sauce gently and serve separately.

Lamb and Aubergine Moussaka

Moussaka is a traditional Greek dish. It needs no more than a salad to accompany it.

SERVES 4

900 g (2 lb) aubergines, thinly sliced
salt and freshly ground pepper
vegetable oil
350 g (12 oz) lean lamb, minced
2 medium onions, skinned and chopped

45 ml (3 tbsp) tomato purée
150 ml ($\frac{1}{4}$ pint) dry white wine
226 g (8 oz) can tomatoes
2.5 ml ($\frac{1}{2}$ tsp) dried oregano
2.5 ml ($\frac{1}{2}$ tsp) dried basil
30 ml (2 tbsp) plain flour
75 g (3 oz) fresh breadcrumbs
15 g ($\frac{1}{2}$ oz) butter
300 ml ($\frac{1}{2}$ pint) milk
75 g (3 oz) Cheddar cheese, grated
1 egg yolk

1. Sprinkle the aubergines generously with salt. Leave in a colander to drain for 30 minutes.

2. Heat 15 ml (1 tbsp) oil in a saucepan, add the lamb and cook quickly until well browned. Stir in the onions, tomato purée, wine, tomatoes, with their juice, herbs and 15 ml (1 tbsp) flour. Bring to the boil, cover and simmer for 30 minutes, then season.

3. Rinse the aubergines, squeeze and pat dry. Heat some oil in a frying pan and fry the aubergine slices, a few at a time, until brown. Drain well on absorbent kitchen paper.

4. Layer the aubergines in a 31 × 25.5 cm (12$\frac{1}{2}$ × 10 inch) shallow ovenproof dish, with the lamb and 50 g (2 oz) breadcrumbs.

5. To make the sauce, melt the butter in a saucepan, stir in the remaining flour and cook gently for 1 minute, stirring. Remove from the heat and gradually stir in the milk. Bring to the boil and continue to cook, stirring, until the sauce thickens. Remove from the heat, then stir in 50 g (2 oz) cheese and the egg yolk.

6. Spoon the sauce over the moussaka and sprinkle with cheese and the remaining bread-crumbs. Bake in the oven at 180°C (350°F) mark 4 for 45 minutes or until golden. Serve immediately.

Pork and Pineapple Casserole

Cooking juices always thicken on standing; this casserole is made with extra liquid to allow for overnight standing and reheating. If you prefer thicker juices after reheating, simply remove the meat with a slotted spoon and boil the liquid rapidly on top of the cooker until reduced.

SERVES 6–8

15 g (½ oz) butter

30 ml (2 tbsp) groundnut or vegetable oil

1.4–1.6 kg (3–3½ lb) boneless pork shoulder, trimmed of excess fat and cut into cubes

60 ml (4 tbsp) brandy

30 ml (2 tbsp) dark soft brown sugar

10 ml (2 tsp) tomato purée

300 ml (½ pint) unsweetened pineapple juice

300 ml (½ pint) chicken stock

1.25 ml (¼ tsp) Tabasco sauce, or to taste

salt and freshly ground pepper

TO SERVE

15 g (½ oz) butter

15 ml (1 tbsp) groundnut or vegetable oil

1 small red pepper, cored, seeded and sliced into thin rings

2 slices of fresh pineapple, cut into neat pieces

1. Melt the butter with the oil in a flameproof casserole, add the pork in batches and fry over moderate to high heat until golden brown on all sides.

2. Return all the meat to the casserole and stir in the brandy, sugar and tomato purée. Mix well, then pour in the pineapple juice and stock. Bring to the boil, stirring, and add the Tabasco and salt and pepper to taste. Cover tightly.

3. Cook at 150°C (300°F) mark 2 for 1½ hours or until the pork is tender, stirring occasionally. Leave in a cold place overnight.

4. To serve, reheat the casserole at 190°C (375°F) mark 5 for 20 minutes or until bubbling.

5. Melt the butter with the oil in a heavy frying pan, add the red pepper rings and toss over high heat for a few minutes or until softened. Add the pineapple pieces and heat through.

6. Remove both pepper and pineapple with a slotted spoon and drain on absorbent kitchen paper. Taste the casserole and adjust the seasoning, then transfer to a warm serving dish and garnish with the red pepper and pineapple.

Likky Pie

This feast-day dish, more grammatically known as Leek Pie, has a delicate subtle flavour.

SERVES 4

225 g (8 oz) leeks, trimmed, sliced and washed

450 g (1 lb) lean boneless pork, cut into 2.5 cm (1 inch) cubes

salt and freshly ground pepper

150 ml (¼ pint) milk

75 ml (3 fl oz) single cream

2 eggs, lightly beaten

225 g (8 oz) packet frozen puff pastry, thawed

1. Parboil the leeks in salted water for about 5 minutes. Drain well. Fill a 26.5 cm (10½ inch) pie plate with the leeks and pork. Season to taste and pour in the milk.

2. Cover with foil and bake at 200°C (400°F) mark 6 for about 1 hour. (Don't worry if it looks curdled.)

3. Stir the cream into the eggs, then pour into the pie. Allow to cool.

4. Roll out the pastry on a lightly floured surface to 5 cm (2 inches) wider than the plate. Cut a 2.5 cm (1 inch) strip from the outer edge and use to line the dampened rim of the pie plate. Dampen the pastry rim with water, cover with the pastry lid and seal the edges well. Knock up and flute. Make a hole in the centre of the pie and use pastry trimmings to decorate.

5. Bake at 220°C (425°F) mark 7 for 25–30 minutes or until risen and golden brown.

Right: Likky pie (above)

Roast Pork with Apples

Crisp crackling is one of the best things about roast pork. To make sure that yours is good and crunchy, score deeply through the skin with a sharp knife, following the natural grain of the meat, then rub in butter and coarse salt before roasting.

SERVES 6–8

1.6 kg (3½ lb) loin of pork

40 g (1½ oz) butter

coarse salt

fresh rosemary sprig

salt and freshly ground pepper

6 large Cox's apples, cored

150 ml (¼ pint) dry white wine (optional)

150 ml (¼ pint) chicken stock

fresh watercress sprigs, to garnish

1. Score the pork rind all over with a sharp knife. Rub with the butter, then sprinkle with coarse salt.

2. Place the rosemary on a rack in a roasting tin, put the pork on top and roast at 180°C (350°F) mark 4 for 2 hours.

3. Season the apples to taste inside and make a shallow cut through the skin around the apples about one-third of the way down. Place in an ovenproof tin or dish and baste with some of the fat from the pork. Cook on a lower shelf in the oven for the last 30 minutes of the cooking time.

4. Remove the pork from the roasting tin and keep it warm on a rack. Drain off most of the fat from the roasting tin, leaving the meat juices. Stir in the wine, if using, loosening the sediment at the bottom of the pan. Boil until almost completely evaporated. Stir in the stock and boil for 2–3 minutes. Strain into a sauceboat.

5. Arrange the apples around the pork, garnish with watercress sprigs and serve accompanied by the hot gravy.

Pork Fillet in Wine and Coriander

Coriander seeds quickly lose their mild, orangy flavour when ground, so try to buy whole seeds to crush yourself.

SERVES 4

700 g (1½ lb) pork fillet (tenderloin), trimmed and cut into 1 cm (½ inch) slices

15 g (½ oz) butter

15 ml (1 tbsp) vegetable oil

1 small green pepper, cored, seeded and sliced into rings

1 medium onion, skinned and chopped

15 g (½ oz) plain flour

15 ml (1 tbsp) coriander seeds, ground

150 ml (¼ pint) chicken stock

150 ml (¼ pint) dry white wine

salt and freshly ground pepper

1. Place the pork between two sheets of grease-proof paper and beat with a mallet or rolling pin until thin.

2. Melt the butter and oil in a large saucepan, add the pork and brown on both sides. Add the pepper and onion and cook lightly for 8–10 minutes or until softened.

3. Stir in the flour and coriander and cook for 1 minute. Gradually add the stock and wine, stirring until the sauce thickens, boils and is smooth. Season to taste. Simmer gently for 5–10 minutes or until the pork is tender and cooked through.

Paupiettes de Veau

Paupiettes are thin slices of meat or fish which are stuffed and rolled. These paupiettes are filled with Parma ham and fresh tarragon and cooked in a subtle wine sauce.

SERVES 4

4 veal escalopes

4 slices of Parma ham

salt and freshly ground pepper

8 fresh tarragon sprigs

seasoned flour

40 g (1½ oz) butter

5 shallots, skinned and finely chopped

150 ml (¼ pint) dry white wine

10 ml (2 tsp) tomato purée

60 ml (4 tbsp) veal stock

fresh tarragon sprigs, to garnish

1. Place the veal escalopes between two sheets of greaseproof paper and beat with a mallet or rolling pin until thin.

2. Lay the escalopes flat and cover with the ham, trimming to fit if necessary. Season and place two tarragon sprigs on each. Roll up and secure with wooden cocktail sticks. Coat lightly in seasoned flour.

3. Melt 25 g (1 oz) of the butter in a sauté pan and fry the shallots and any ham trimmings until the shallots are soft. Add the veal rolls and fry until evenly browned all over.

4. Stir in the wine, tomato purée and stock. Season to taste. Cover the pan tightly and cook over gentle heat for 20 minutes or until tender.

5. Transfer the veal rolls to a warmed serving dish and remove the cocktail sticks. Keep hot.

6. Boil the pan juices until reduced and thickened. Taste and adjust the seasoning. Stir in the remaining butter, heat until melted, then pour over the veal rolls. Garnish and serve.

Creamed Kidneys in Wine

Use lambs' kidneys, which are the smallest available and always juicy and tender, in this very speedy dish.

SERVES 4

25 g (1 oz) butter

12 lambs' kidneys, halved and cored

225 g (8 oz) mushrooms, sliced

3 celery sticks, diced

1 medium onion, skinned and finely chopped

25 g (1 oz) plain flour

300 ml (½ pint) dry red wine

5 ml (1 tsp) mustard powder

salt and freshly ground pepper

150 ml (¼ pint) double cream

1. Melt the butter in a medium saucepan. Add the kidneys, mushrooms, celery and onion and fry gently for 10 minutes or until tender.

2. Stir in the flour and cook for 1–2 minutes. Gradually stir in the wine, mustard and salt and pepper. Cook for a further 5 minutes. Stir in the cream and reheat gently.

Above: Paupiettes de veau (page 53)
Right: Calves' liver with green grapes and Madiera
(page 57)

Fillet of Veal with Champagne Sauce and Courgettes

Prepare the caramelised strips of lemon rind the day before, if wished, but take care not to brown them as they cook.

SERVES 4

thinly pared rind of 3 lemons, cut into fine strips

15 ml (1 tbsp) sugar

175 g (6 oz) unsalted butter

750 g (1½ lb) fillet of veal

salt and white pepper

450 ml (¾ pint) Champagne or other sparkling dry white wine

300 ml (½ pint) veal stock

4–6 courgettes, cut lengthways into thin slices

fresh chervil sprigs, to garnish

1. Put the strips of lemon rind into a saucepan of boiling water and boil for 1 minute. Drain and refresh under cold running water.

2. Dissolve the sugar in 90 ml (6 tbsp) water. Add the lemon rind strips and boil until the liquid has evaporated and the lemon rind is caramelised. Remove from the heat immediately as the lemon must not brown. Set aside.

3. Heat 50 g (2 oz) of the butter in a heavy flameproof casserole in which the veal will just fit. Add the veal and sear evenly all over. Season, then transfer to the oven. Roast at 220°C (425°F) mark 7 for 15 minutes. (The veal will remain pink in the centre.)

4. Transfer the veal to a warmed plate, cover and keep warm. Tip any excess fat from the casserole, then stir in the wine, dislodging any sediment. Bring to the boil and reduce to 90 ml (6 tbsp). Stir in the stock and boil to reduce to 175 ml (6 fl oz).

5. Meanwhile, steam the courgettes for about 2 minutes or until tender but still crisp.

6. Strain the sauce into a clean saucepan and reheat gently. Over a low heat, gradually whisk in the remaining butter, cut into small pieces, making sure each piece is fully incorporated before adding the next. Season and keep warm over a low heat. Do not allow the sauce to boil.

7. Carve the veal into neat slices. Spoon the sauce on to four warmed plates. Place the veal on top and arrange the courgette slices neatly around. Garnish with the caramelised lemon rind strips and sprigs of chervil.

Veal Sweetbreads with Red and Yellow Peppers

The fresh taste of the peppers contrasts well with the smooth texture of the sweetbreads and the cream sauce in this dish.

SERVES 4

450 g (1 lb) veal sweetbreads

slice of lemon

40 g (1½ oz) butter, chilled

1 carrot, diced

1 celery stick, diced

1 leek, diced

2 garlic cloves, skinned and chopped

1 bay leaf

sprig of fresh thyme

few parsley sprigs

150 ml (¼ pint) chicken stock

15 ml (1 tbsp) brandy

5 ml (1 tsp) oil

1 red pepper, cored, seeded and cut into julienne strips

1 yellow pepper, cored, seeded and cut into julienne strips

salt and freshly ground pepper

5 ml (1 tsp) chopped fresh parsley

5 ml (1 tsp) chopped fresh chives

1. Wash the sweetbreads well, then place them in a saucepan of cold water with the slice of lemon. Bring to the boil, then simmer for 3 minutes. Drain and cool, then carefully remove any skin.

2. Melt 15 g ($\frac{1}{2}$ oz) of the butter in a saucepan and fry the carrot, celery, leek and garlic until soft. Add the bay leaf, thyme and parsley sprigs, and arrange the sweetbreads on top of the bed of vegetables.

3. Pour over the stock. Bring to a simmer, then cover and cook for about 20 minutes or until firm and tender. Carefully remove the sweetbreads from the pan.

4. Strain the stock and return it to the rinsed-out pan. Add the brandy and boil rapidly for about 2 minutes or until the sauce is slightly syrupy. Return the sweetbreads to the pan and simmer very gently to warm through.

5. Heat the oil in a frying pan and stir-fry the peppers for 2 minutes. Season to taste.

6. Spoon the peppers on to a serving plate. Cut the sweetbreads into thick slices and arrange on top of the peppers. Whisk the remaining butter into the sauce. Stir in the chopped parsley and chives, taste and adjust the seasoning. Pour over the sweetbreads and serve at once.

Calf's Liver with Green Grapes and Madeira

Seasoned with sage and served with a slightly sweet sauce, calf's liver is a delicious, light main course. Serve with rice.

SERVES 4

50 g (2 oz) butter

50 g (2 oz) onion or shallot, skinned and finely chopped

175 ml (6 fl oz) chicken stock

100 ml (4 fl oz) Madeira

salt and freshly ground pepper

24 large green grapes, peeled, halved and seeded

4 slices of calf's liver—each weighing about 75–100 g (3–4 oz), trimmed

4 sage leaves, thinly sliced

4 sage sprigs, to garnish

1. Melt half the butter in a frying pan and fry the onion until golden. Add the stock and Madeira, season and bring to the boil. Boil rapidly for 4–5 minutes or until reduced and of a slightly syrupy consistency. Add the grape halves and warm through gently. Taste and adjust the seasoning.

2. Melt the remaining butter in a large frying pan. Season the liver, and fry with the sliced sage leaves for 3–5 minutes, turning once.

3. Remove the liver from the pan and serve at once with the Madeira sauce. Garnish with sprigs of fresh sage.

Overleaf: Roast beef and Yorkshire pudding (page 61), Brussels sprouts with chestnuts (page 60)

SUNDAY LUNCH

Parsnip and Apple Soup

The velvety texture of a creamy soup is always welcoming, and the unmistakable flavour of parsnips, blended with a hint of tart cooking apple, is very warming.

SERVES 6–8

25 g (1 oz) butter
700 g (1½ lb) parsnips, peeled and roughly chopped
1 Bramley cooking apple, cored, peeled and roughly chopped
1.1 litres (2 pints) chicken stock
4 fresh sage leaves or 2.5 ml (½ tsp) dried sage
2 cloves
150 ml (¼ pint) single cream
salt and freshly ground pepper
fresh sage leaves or parsley and croûtons, to garnish

1. Melt the butter in a large saucepan, add the parsnips and apple, cover and cook gently for 10 minutes, stirring occasionally.
2. Pour in the stock and add the sage and cloves. Bring to the boil, cover, then simmer for 30 minutes or until the parsnip is softened.
3. Remove the sage leaves and cloves, leave to cool slightly, then purée the soup in a blender or food processor.
4. Return to the saucepan and reheat gently with the cream. Season to taste. Serve hot, garnished with the sage or parsley and croûtons.

Brussels Sprouts with Chestnuts

Brussels sprouts and chestnuts are a delicious combination. Peeling the chestnuts is a fiddly job, which can be done in advance. Take care when peeling the hot chestnuts not to burn your fingers.

SERVES 6–8

550 g (1¼ lb) fresh chestnuts
1.1 kg (2½ lb) Brussels sprouts, trimmed
40 g (1½ oz) butter
freshly ground pepper

1. With the point of a small sharp knife, make a small cut on the flat side of each chestnut.
2. Bake the nuts in their skins in the oven at 200°C (400°F) mark 6 for 20 minutes, then peel off the outer shell and the inner skin. (They are easier to peel while hot.)
3. Meanwhile, cook the Brussels sprouts in boiling salted water for 8–10 minutes or until just tender. Drain.
4. Over a high heat, toss the chestnuts and Brussels sprouts with the butter and pepper to taste, until the butter is melted. Serve at once.

Roast Beef and Yorkshire Pudding

All over Britain this is recognised as a traditional dish, especially for Sunday lunch. Using semi-skimmed instead of whole milk will produce the same effect as using half milk and half water in the Yorkshire pudding batter.

SERVES 6–8

sirloin, rib, rump or topside of beef (allow 175 g/6 oz off the bone per person; 225–350 g/8–12 oz on the bone per person)

25 g (1 oz) beef dripping (optional)

freshly ground pepper

5 ml (1 tsp) mustard powder (optional)

prepared English mustard or horseradish sauce, to serve

FOR THE YORKSHIRE PUDDING

100 g (4 oz) plain flour

pinch of salt

1 egg

200 ml (7 fl oz) milk

FOR THE GRAVY

10 ml (2 tsp) plain flour

300 ml ($\frac{1}{2}$ pint) beef stock

salt and freshly ground pepper

1. Weigh the meat and calculate the cooking time: for rare beef allow 15 minutes per 450 g (1 lb) plus 15 minutes; for medium beef allow 20 minutes per 450 g (1 lb) plus 20 minutes; and for well-done beef allow 25 minutes per 450 g (1 lb) plus 25 minutes.

2. Put the meat into a shallow roasting tin, preferably on a roasting rack, with the thickest layer of fat uppermost and the cut sides exposed to the heat. Add dripping if the meat is lean. Season the meat with pepper and mustard powder, if wished.

3. Roast at 180°C (350°F) mark 4 for the calculated time, basting occasionally with the juices from the tin.

4. Meanwhile, to make the Yorkshire pudding batter, mix the flour and salt in a bowl, then make a well in the centre and break in the egg.

5. Add half the milk and, using a wooden spoon, gradually work in the flour. Beat the mixture until it is smooth, then add the remaining milk and 75 ml (3 fl oz) water. Beat until well mixed and the surface is covered with tiny bubbles.

6. Forty-five minutes before the end of the cooking time, cover the joint with foil and place on the bottom shelf of the oven. Increase the oven temperature to 220°C (425°F) mark 7.

7. Put 30 ml (2 tbsp) fat from the beef into a baking tin and place in the oven until the fat is very hot. Pour in the Yorkshire pudding batter and return to the oven to cook for 40–45 minutes or until risen and golden brown. Do not open the oven door for 30 minutes.

8. After 30 minutes, transfer the cooked meat to a warmed serving plate, cover and leave to rest for 20 minutes before carving.

9. To make the gravy, the meat juices alone may be used. For a thicker gravy, skim some of the fat from the surface and place the roasting tin over moderate heat. Sprinkle the flour into the tin and stir it into the pan juices, scraping up the brown sediment.

10. Cook over high heat, stirring constantly, until the flour has browned slightly. (When the meat is carved, any juices from the meat can be added to the gravy.) Add up to 300 ml ($\frac{1}{2}$ pint) of beef stock to the tin and stir well. Bring to the boil, simmer for 2–3 minutes and season to taste. Pour into a warmed gravyboat or jug.

11. Serve the carved beef with the Yorkshire pudding, cut into portions. Accompany with the gravy and mustard or horseradish sauce.

VARIATION

For individual Yorkshire puddings or pop-overs, use 50 g (2 oz) plain flour, a pinch of salt, 1 egg and 150 ml ($\frac{1}{4}$ pint) milk and water mixed. Cook for 15–20 minutes. This quantity will fill 12 patty tins.

Creamed Potato Gratin

This potato dish goes very well with all roast meat and game. The potatoes can be mashed and put into their dish, ready for baking, well in advance, but add the cream and cheese only just before putting the dish into the oven.

SERVES 6–8

1.4 kg (3 lb) potatoes, peeled
75 g (3 oz) butter
75 ml (3 fl oz) milk
salt and freshly ground pepper
75 ml (3 fl oz) double cream
50 g (2 oz) Parmesan cheese, freshly grated

1. Cook the potatoes in boiling salted water until tender. Drain well and return to the pan. Mash the potatoes with a potato masher, then beat in the butter and milk to make a creamy mixture. Season well with salt and pepper. Pipe the potatoes into a large ovenproof dish.

2. Pour the double cream evenly over the potatoes, then sprinkle with the grated cheese. About 1 hour before the beef has finished cooking, put the potatoes into the oven, with the beef, on the top shelf.

3. After about 15 minutes, cover the beef with foil and move it to the bottom shelf of the oven. Increase the oven temperature to 220°C (425°F) mark 7. Continue cooking the potatoes in the oven with the Yorkshire pudding until the top is browned.

Iced Rose Petal Soufflés

You can either make individual soufflés or one large one. Do not make more than two or three days in advance.

SERVES 6–8

50 g (2 oz) well-scented rose petals, dried
100 g (4 oz) caster sugar
200 g (7 oz) fromage blanc
75 g (3 oz) crème fraîche
4 egg whites
few drops of rose-water (optional)
small rose petals, to decorate

1. Tie a collar of double thickness greaseproof paper around six or eight individual soufflé or ramekin dishes.

2. Put the rose petals in a blender or food processor with the sugar and blend until the petals are reduced to very small pieces.

3. Blend the fromage blanc and crème fraîche together. Whisk the egg whites until stiff but not dry. Taste and add a few drops of rose-water to increase the flavour, if necessary.

4. Gently fold the egg whites into the fromage blanc mixture with the sugared rose petals.

5. Divide the mixture between the dishes. Freeze until firm, then cover the tops.

6. About 25 minutes before serving, carefully remove the collars from the soufflés. Leave the soufflés in the refrigerator until required. Serve decorated with small rose petals.

Right: Chicken with apricots and brandy (page 64)

POULTRY AND GAME

Chicken with Apricots and Brandy

This delicious chicken dish combines a number of unexpected flavours most successfully.
SERVES 4–6

4–6 chicken breast fillets, with skin on
45 ml (3 tbsp) plain flour, plus extra for dusting
100 g (4 oz) butter
60 ml (4 tbsp) dry white wine or cider
15–30 ml (1–2 tbsp) brandy (optional)
100 g (4 oz) streaky bacon, rinded and chopped
100 g (4 oz) mushrooms, wiped and sliced
100 g (4 oz) onion, skinned and chopped
300 ml ($\frac{1}{2}$ pint) chicken stock
salt and freshly ground pepper
3 juniper berries (optional)
100 g (4 oz) no-soak dried apricots
1 bay leaf
4–6 thick round slices of bread
150 ml ($\frac{1}{4}$ pint) single cream
fresh parsley, to garnish

1. Dust the chicken with flour. Melt 40 g ($1\frac{1}{2}$ oz) butter in a frying pan and gently brown the chicken on all sides, then remove to a casserole.
2. Add the wine and brandy, if using, to the pan, bring to the boil, pour over the chicken.
3. Melt a further 40 g ($1\frac{1}{2}$ oz) butter in the pan and fry the bacon, mushrooms and onion slowly until the onion is soft and starting to brown. Blend in 45 ml (3 tbsp) flour and gradually stir in the stock. Season well and add the juniper berries, if using, the apricots and the bay leaf.
4. Pour the sauce over the chicken, cover and cook in the oven at 170°C (325°F) mark 3 for about $1\frac{1}{2}$ hours or until tender.

5. Melt remaining butter in the pan. Fry the bread until crisp. Drain and keep hot.
6. When the chicken is cooked, remove from the casserole and keep hot. Remove the bay leaf, then rub the sauce through a sieve or purée in a blender or food processor. Add the cream, adjust seasoning and reheat without boiling.
7. Arrange a chicken breast on each croûton and place on a warm platter. Spoon over some sauce. Garnish with parsley. Serve the remaining sauce separately.

Chicken with Tarragon Mayonnaise

It is important to use fresh tarragon in this dish: dried tarragon is a poor substitute.
SERVES 6

6 chicken breast fillets, skinned
2 celery sticks, sliced
200 ml (7 fl oz) dry white wine
30 ml (2 tbsp) chopped fresh tarragon
salt and freshly ground pepper
300 ml ($\frac{1}{2}$ pint) lemon mayonnaise
tarragon sprigs, to garnish

1. Put the chicken in a frying pan. Add celery, wine, tarragon, salt and pepper. Bring to the boil, then reduce the heat, cover and simmer for 20–30 minutes or until tender. Leave to cool.
2. When cool, strain the juices into a pan and boil rapidly until reduced to 90 ml (6 tbsp). Leave to cool.
3. Arrange the chicken on a plate. Stir the reduced juices into the mayonnaise and spoon over the chicken. Garnish with tarragon.

Chicken in Red Wine with Raisins

This is a medieval recipe, originally intended for rabbit, but equally good with chicken. The sauce is spicy and sweetish, and is used to marinate the meat and fruits before cooking.

SERVES 4

300 ml (½ pint) red wine

45 ml (3 tbsp) red wine vinegar

100 g (4 oz) seedless raisins

175 g (6 oz) no-soak dried apricots, halved

5 ml (1 tsp) ground ginger

5 ml (1 tsp) ground cinnamon

1 cm (½ inch) piece of fresh root ginger, peeled and grated

4 cloves

4 juniper berries, lightly crushed

4 chicken breast fillets, with skin on, each weighing about 175 g (6 oz)

30 ml (2 tbsp) plain wholemeal flour

salt and freshly ground pepper

15 g (½ oz) butter

15 ml (1 tbsp) vegetable oil

300 ml (½ pint) chicken stock

orange segments, to garnish

1. Put the wine, vinegar, raisins, apricots, ground ginger, cinnamon, fresh ginger, cloves and juniper berries in a dish. Add the chicken breasts and spoon the liquid over them. Cover and leave to marinate in a cool place for 3–4 hours or overnight.

2. Remove the chicken from the marinade (reserving the marinade) and dry with absorbent kitchen paper. Coat in the flour, seasoned with salt and pepper. Heat the butter and oil in a large flameproof casserole, add the chicken, skin side down, and fry until lightly browned. Turn over and fry the other side. Drain on absorbent kitchen paper.

3. Pour off any excess fat from the casserole, then stir in the chicken stock and the reserved marinade and fruit and bring to the boil. Return the chicken to the casserole, cover tightly and cook for about 30 minutes or until the chicken is tender.

4. Transfer the chicken to a warmed serving plate and keep warm. Boil the liquid until reduced and thickened, then pour over the chicken. Serve garnished with orange segments.

Coronation Chicken

This famous chicken dish is perfect for a summer buffet party.

SERVES 8

2.3 kg (5 lb) chicken, cooked

25 g (1 oz) butter

1 small onion, skinned and finely chopped

15 ml (1 tbsp) curry paste

15 ml (1 tbsp) tomato purée

100 ml (4 fl oz) red wine

1 bay leaf

juice of ½ lemon

4 canned apricots, drained and finely chopped

300 ml (½ pint) mayonnaise

150 ml (¼ pint) whipping cream

salt and freshly ground pepper

cucumber slices, to garnish

1. Remove all the meat from the chicken and dice.

2. Heat the butter in a small pan, add the onion and cook for 3 minutes or until softened. Add the curry paste, tomato purée, wine, bay leaf and lemon juice.

3. Simmer, uncovered, for about 10 minutes or until well reduced. Strain and cool.

4. Sieve the chopped apricot to produce a purée. Beat the cooked sauce into the mayonnaise with the apricot purée.

5. Whip the cream until softly stiff and fold into the mixture. Season, adding a little more lemon juice if necessary.

6. Toss the chicken pieces in the sauce, transfer to a serving dish and garnish with cucumber.

Chicken and Broccoli Pie

The sauce in this recipe uses plain wholemeal flour and is delicately flavoured with just a hint of lemon. For variation, you could top the pie with wholemeal shortcrust pastry.

SERVES 4–6

25 g (1 oz) butter

2 carrots, diced

8 button onions, skinned

100 g (4 oz) button mushrooms, wiped

25 g (1 oz) plain wholemeal flour

450 ml (¾ pint) milk, plus extra to glaze

450 g (1 lb) boneless cooked chicken, cut into strips

175 g (6 oz) broccoli, blanched

grated rind of ½ lemon

30 ml (2 tbsp) single cream

salt and freshly ground pepper

225 g (8 oz) packet frozen puff pastry, thawed

1. Melt the butter in a large saucepan and lightly fry the carrots, onions and mushrooms for 8 minutes, stirring occasionally.

2. Stir in the flour and cook for 1–2 minutes. Gradually add the milk, stirring continuously until the sauce thickens, boils and is smooth. Simmer for 3–4 minutes.

3. Add the chicken, broccoli, lemon rind and cream to the sauce. Season to taste and pour into a 26.5 cm (10½ inch) pie plate.

4. Roll out the pastry on a lightly floured surface to 5 cm (2 inches) wider all round than the plate. Cut a 2.5 cm (1 inch) strip from the outer edge and position on the dampened rim of the plate. Dampen with water and place the pastry lid on top. Trim and press down well to seal. Finally, knock up and flute the edges. Use pastry trimmings to decorate and make a hole in the top of the pie. Brush the pastry with milk to glaze.

5. Bake at 200°C (400°F) mark 6 for 25 minutes or until golden brown. Serve at once.

Chicken and Stilton Roulades

For this unusual dish, tender chicken breast fillets are flattened and spread with a rich butter and blue cheese mixture before being rolled in bacon.

SERVES 4

100 g (4 oz) Blue Stilton cheese, crumbled

75 g (3 oz) butter, softened

4 chicken breast fillets, skinned

8 rashers of smoked back bacon, rinded

15 ml (1 tbsp) vegetable oil

25 g (1 oz) butter

1 glass of red wine made up to 300 ml (½ pint) with chicken stock

salt and freshly ground pepper

5 ml (1 tsp) arrowroot

parsley or thyme sprigs, to garnish

1. Put the cheese and softened butter in a bowl and beat to a smooth paste.

2. Put the chicken breasts between two sheets of damp greaseproof paper and beat with a mallet or rolling pin until thin. Spread the butter mixture evenly on one side of each breast.

3. Roll up the chicken breasts and wrap each one in two bacon rashers. Secure with wooden cocktail sticks.

4. Heat the oil and remaining butter in a heavy-based pan and brown the chicken rolls well.

5. Pour in the red wine and stock, season, bring to the boil, cover and simmer gently for 35–40 minutes or until tender, turning occasionally.

6. Remove the chicken from the pan with a slotted spoon. Remove the cocktail sticks, place the chicken in a serving dish and keep warm.

7. Blend the arrowroot with a little water until smooth and pour into the pan juices. Heat, stirring, until thickened. Season and spoon the sauce over the chicken. Garnish with herbs.

Right: Chicken and Stilton roulades (above)

Roast Turkey with Parsley and Lemon Stuffing

The trick when roasting a turkey is to keep the breast meat moist while the darker meat on the legs, which takes longer to cook, is finishing off. To do this, cover the breast with streaky bacon rashers, baste well from time to time and protect it with foil if it shows signs of becoming too brown.

3.6–5 kg (8–11¼ lb) turkey serves 10–15
5–6.8 kg (11¼–15 lb) turkey serves 15–20
6.8–9 kg (15–20¼ lb) turkey serves 20–30

25 g (1 oz) butter
2 medium onions, skinned and finely chopped
2 celery sticks, finely chopped
225 g (8 oz) fresh wholemeal breadcrumbs
60 ml (4 tbsp) chopped fresh parsley
finely grated rind of 2 lemons
salt and freshly ground pepper
1 egg, beaten
1 oven-ready turkey, thawed if frozen
streaky bacon rashers

1. To make the stuffing, melt the butter in a large saucepan, add the onions and celery, cover and cook gently for about 10 minutes or until really soft, stirring occasionally.

2. Remove from the heat and add the breadcrumbs, parsley and lemon rind. Season and stir in the egg.

3. Wash the inside of the bird and stuff at the neck end before folding the neck skin over. Make the turkey plump and as even in shape as possible, then truss it with the wings folded under the body and the legs tied together.

4. Weigh the turkey and calculate the cooking time, allowing 20 minutes per 450 g (1 lb) plus 20 minutes.

5. Place the turkey in a roasting tin, then sprinkle with salt and pepper.

6. Place the streaky bacon rashers over the breast to prevent it from becoming dry. Roast at 180°C (350°F) mark 4, basting occasionally. Put a piece of foil over the bird if necessary.

7. Leave the turkey to rest for 10 minutes before carving.

Turkey Escalopes with Plums

This is a very quick dish to cook, but you do need to plan ahead and let the meat marinate overnight, or at least for a few hours, for maximum flavour.
SERVES 4

2 turkey breast fillets, each weighing about 225 g (8 oz), skinned and cut widthways into 5 cm (2 inch) slices
75 ml (3 fl oz) unsweetened apple juice
45 ml (3 tbsp) soy sauce
45 ml (3 tbsp) dry sherry
1 small garlic clove, skinned and crushed
5 ml (1 tsp) chopped fresh thyme or 1.25 ml (¼ tsp) dried thyme
15 g (½ oz) butter
15 ml (1 tbsp) vegetable oil
225 g (8 oz) plums or damsons, halved and stoned
freshly ground pepper
fresh thyme sprigs, to garnish

1. Put the turkey slices between two sheets of damp greaseproof paper and beat with a mallet or rolling pin until about 2.5 cm (1 inch) thick.

2. Place in a large shallow dish and pour over the apple juice, soy sauce, sherry, garlic and thyme. Cover and leave in the refrigerator to marinate for 3–4 hours or overnight.

3. Remove the turkey from the marinade, reserving the marinade. Heat the butter and oil in a large frying pan and quickly fry the turkey until browned on both sides. Add the plums, reserved marinade and pepper to taste.

4. Cover and simmer gently for 10–15 minutes or until tender, stirring occasionally. Garnish with thyme before serving.

Poacher's Pie

*If wild rabbit is not available, use commercially
produced meat, on sale in many supermarkets.*
SERVES 4

225 g (8 oz) plain flour

salt and freshly ground pepper

50 g (2 oz) butter, diced

50 g (2 oz) lard, diced

450 g (1 lb) boneless rabbit, skinned and cubed

100 g (4 oz) streaky bacon rashers, rinded and
chopped

2 medium potatoes, peeled and sliced

1 medium leek, trimmed, sliced and washed

15 ml (1 tbsp) chopped fresh parsley

1.25 ml (¼ tsp) mixed dried herbs

chicken stock

1 egg, beaten, to glaze

1. Put the flour and a pinch of salt into a bowl
and rub in the butter and lard until the mixture
resembles fine breadcrumbs. Add 45–60 ml
(3–4 tbsp) cold water and mix to a firm dough.
2. Fill a 26.5 cm (10½ inch) pie plate with alternate layers of rabbit, bacon and vegetables,
sprinkling with seasoning and herbs. Half-fill
with stock.
3. Roll out the pastry on a lightly floured
surface to 5 cm (2 inches) wider than the top of
the plate. Cut a 2.5 cm (1 inch) strip from the
outer edge and line the dampened rim of the
plate. Dampen the pastry rim and cover with the
pastry lid. Trim and seal the edges. Make a hole
in the centre to let the steam escape. Decorate
with pastry leaves and brush with egg.
4. Bake in the oven at 190°C (375°F) mark 5 for
30 minutes. Cover loosely with foil, then reduce
to 180°C (350°F) mark 4 for a further hour.

Rabbit Cider Hot Pot

*One medium-sized rabbit, jointed, should weigh
about 1.1 kg (2½ lb). If you are using smaller joints
to make up this total weight, cut down the cooking
time accordingly.*
SERVES 4

6 rabbit joints, total weight about 1.1 kg (2½ lb)

12 prunes

450 ml (15 fl oz) can dry cider

2 medium onions, skinned and sliced

30 ml (2 tbsp) wholegrain mustard

4 bay leaves

salt and freshly ground pepper

60 ml (4 tbsp) plain flour

30 ml (2 tbsp) vegetable oil

15 g (½ oz) butter

450 g (1 lb) parsnips, peeled and cut into chunks

397 g (14 oz) can red kidney beans, drained

1. Rinse and dry the rabbit joints. Put in a large
bowl with the prunes, cider, onions, mustard,
bay leaves and 450 ml (¾ pint) water. Season,
then stir gently to mix. Cover tightly and refrigerate overnight.
2. The next day, lift the rabbit joints out of the
marinade and dry. Reserve the marinade. Toss
the rabbit joints in flour. Heat the oil and butter
in a large flameproof casserole, add the joints
and fry until brown.
3. Sprinkle any remaining flour into the
casserole. Pour in the marinade, reserving the
prunes. Add the parsnips. Bring to the boil and
cover tightly.
4. Cook at 180°C (350°F) mark 4 for about 40
minutes. Add the prunes and beans, cover again
and cook for a further 20–30 minutes or until
everything is tender.

Turkey in Spiced Yogurt

To enjoy their evocative flavours at their best, spices should be bought in small quantities and used quickly. This flavoursome dish needs no more than plain boiled rice to accompany it.

SERVES 6

about 1.1 kg (2½ lb) turkey leg meat on the bone

7.5 ml (1½ tsp) ground cumin

7.5 ml (1½ tsp) ground coriander

2.5 ml (½ tsp) ground turmeric

2.5 ml (½ tsp) ground ginger

salt and freshly ground pepper

300 ml (½ pint) natural yogurt

30 ml (2 tbsp) lemon juice

45 ml (3 tbsp) vegetable oil

225 g (8 oz) onion, skinned and sliced

45 ml (3 tbsp) desiccated coconut

30 ml (2 tbsp) plain flour

150 ml (¼ pint) chicken stock or water

chopped fresh parsley, to garnish

1. Cut the turkey meat off the bone into large fork-sized pieces, discarding the skin. There should be about 900 g (2 lb) meat.

2. In a large bowl, mix the spices with the seasoning, yogurt and lemon juice. Stir well until evenly blended.

3. Fold the yogurt mixture through the turkey meat until well coated. Cover tightly with cling film and refrigerate for several hours.

4. Heat the oil in a medium flameproof casserole, add the onion and cook until lightly browned. Add the coconut and flour and fry gently, stirring, for about 1 minute.

5. Remove from the heat and stir in the turkey with its marinade and the stock. Return to the heat and bring slowly to the boil, stirring all the time. Cover tightly and cook in the oven at 170°C (325°F) mark 3 for 1–1¼ hours or until the turkey is tender.

6. Taste and adjust the seasoning and serve garnished with parsley.

Turkey Breasts with Asparagus

Choose thin sprue asparagus for this dish. The tips are deliciously succulent and tender.

SERVES 4

225 g (8 oz) thin (sprue) asparagus stalks

2 turkey breast fillets, each weighing about 225 g (8 oz), skinned and halved

30 ml (2 tbsp) plain flour

salt and freshly ground pepper

15 g (½ oz) butter

15 ml (1 tbsp) vegetable oil

300 ml (½ pint) chicken stock

5 ml (1 tsp) chopped fresh sage or 2.5 ml (½ tsp) dried sage

60 ml (4 tbsp) dry white wine

150 ml (¼ pint) soured cream

1. Cut off the ends of the asparagus if they are tough and woody. Trim them all to the same length, cut off the tips and cut the stalks into three pieces each.

2. Place the turkey breast pieces between two sheets of damp greaseproof paper and bat out slightly with a rolling pin or meat mallet. Coat in the flour seasoned with salt and pepper, shaking off any excess.

3. Heat the butter and oil in a large frying pan and fry the turkey until lightly browned on both sides. Add the chicken stock, asparagus stalks, sage and wine, cover and cook gently for 15–20 minutes or until tender.

4. Five minutes before the end of the cooking time, add the asparagus tips and the cream. Season to taste.

Right: Turkey escalopes with plums (page 68)

Salmagundi

Salmagundi has been a popular cold dish for centuries, often incorporating other cold meats, fish and a variety of vegetables. This recipe can be made using chicken only, leaving out the duck. Select firm-textured vegetables and arrange the ingredients in ever-widening circles to create an attractive effect.

SERVES 8

1 oven-ready duckling, weighing about 2.3 kg (5 lb), thawed if frozen

salt and freshly ground pepper

1 oven-ready chicken, weighing about 2 kg (4½ lb), thawed if frozen

450 g (1 lb) carrots, cut into 0.5 cm (¼ inch) wide strips

450 g (1 lb) potatoes, peeled

150 ml (¼ pint) vegetable oil

75 ml (5 tbsp) lemon juice

pinch of mustard powder

pinch of sugar

450 g (1 lb) shelled peas, cooked

1 cucumber, sliced

225 g (8 oz) tomatoes, thinly sliced

4 celery sticks, thinly sliced

4 eggs, hard-boiled (optional)

mayonnaise (optional)

slices of stuffed olives and radishes, to garnish

1. Weigh the duckling, prick the skin all over with a skewer or sharp fork and sprinkle with salt. Place, breast side down, on a rack or trivet in a roasting tin. Roast in the top of the oven at 200°C (400°F) mark 6, basting occasionally, for 20 minutes per 450 g (1 lb).

2. Weigh the chicken and sprinkle with salt and pepper. Place in a shallow roasting tin and roast below the duck on the lowest shelf of the oven for 20 minutes per 450 g (1 lb) plus 20 minutes. Leave the chicken and the duck to cool for 1–2 hours or until cool enough to handle.

3. Using a sharp knife, make a slit along each side of the breastbone of both the chicken and duck. Remove and discard the skin.

4. Carefully remove all the flesh from the carcasses of both birds. Discard the carcasses and cut the flesh into thin strips, about 5 cm (2 inches) long.

5. Cook the carrots in boiling salted water for 8 minutes or until just tender. Drain and rinse in cold water. Cook the potatoes in boiling salted water for 15 minutes or until tender. Drain and leave to cool, then dice finely.

6. Make the dressing by whisking the oil, lemon juice, mustard and sugar together with salt and pepper to taste.

7. Choose a large oval platter for making up the salmagundi. Place the potato and peas in the bottom of the dish to give a flat base. Arrange the carrot strips or a layer of cucumber on top, following the oval shape of the platter.

8. Pour over a little dressing. Next, arrange a layer of cucumber or carrot, slightly inside the first layer so that it may easily be seen.

9. Top with more layers of chicken meat, peas, tomato slices, celery and duck meat. Make each layer smaller than the previous one so that the lower layers can all be seen. Sprinkle each one with dressing. Continue layering until all the ingredients are used.

10. If using the eggs, shell and halve them, then top each half with a little mayonnaise, if used. Garnish with a few slices of stuffed olive and radish, arranged round the edge of the dish.

Loin of Venison with Cranberries and Glazed Apples

The venison stock can be made at least two days in advance and kept in a cool place. The cranberries can also be cooked a day or two in advance, and drained of their liquid some time before serving.

SERVES 8

two 750 g (1½ lb) loins of venison, bones and trimmings reserved

3 carrots, chopped

2 celery sticks, chopped

3 small leeks, chopped

16 juniper berries, crushed

pared rind of 1 orange

bouquet garni of 3 fresh thyme sprigs, 1 fresh rosemary sprig, 1 bay leaf and 6 fresh parsley stalks tied together

salt and freshly ground pepper

1 bottle of fruity red wine

100 g (4 oz) butter

100 g (4 oz) cranberries

75 g (3 oz) caster sugar

50 ml (2 fl oz) Calvados

50 ml (2 fl oz) dry muscat wine

3 crisp green dessert apples, cored and sliced

1. Put the venison bones and trimmings in a roasting tin and brown under a hot grill. Add the vegetables and brown these lightly.

2. Tip the bones and vegetables into a large saucepan and add the juniper berries, orange rind, bouquet garni and seasoning.

3. Stir half the red wine into the roasting tin and bring to the boil, stirring to mix in the sediment. Pour this wine into the saucepan and add 1.35 litres (2¼ pints) water.

4. Bring to the boil, skimming the scum from the surface, and simmer for about 2½ hours. Skim off the scum occasionally.

5. Leave to cool, then remove the fat from the surface. Strain the stock, pressing down well to extract as much liquid from the vegetables and flavourings as possible, but do not press the vegetables through the sieve. Stir the remaining red wine into the stock and boil until reduced to 750 ml (1¼ pints).

6. Heat half the butter in a roasting tin, add the loins of venison and sear evenly all over. Transfer to the oven and roast at 220°C (425°F) mark 7 for 15–20 minutes; they will remain pink inside.

7. Meanwhile, put the cranberries into a saucepan and pour 75 ml (3 fl oz) boiling water over. Cover and leave to soak for 5 minutes. Bring to simmering point and simmer for 3 minutes. Remove from the heat and leave for 5 minutes, then stir in 25 g (1 oz) of the sugar. Set aside.

8. Remove the venison from the roasting tin to a carving board, cover and keep warm.

9. Heat the Calvados and muscat wine in a saucepan to simmering point. Stir in the remaining sugar, then add the apples. Lower the heat and poach for about 3 minutes. Remove from the heat.

10. Gently reheat the red wine sauce and gradually swirl in the remaining butter, cut into small pieces. Season. Keep warm, but do not allow the sauce to boil.

11. Cut each loin of venison into 12 or 16 slices. Spoon the sauce over a large, warmed platter and place the venison on top. Remove the cranberries and apples from their liquid with a slotted spoon. Use to garnish the serving platter. Serve the slices with some cranberries and apples and the sauce spooned round.

Venison Escalopes with Red Wine

You can buy venison from any butcher with a game licence. Young venison is usually tender enough not to need hanging but older, tougher animals benefit from it. Your butcher can advise on this.

SERVES 6

6 escalopes of venison cut from the haunch (leg), each weighing about 175 g (6 oz)

1 small onion, skinned and finely chopped

1 bay leaf

2 fresh parsley sprigs

8 juniper berries

300 ml ($\frac{1}{2}$ pint) dry red wine

15 g ($\frac{1}{2}$ oz) butter

15 ml (1 tbsp) vegetable oil

30 ml (2 tbsp) redcurrant jelly

salt and freshly ground pepper

1. Put the escalopes in a large shallow dish and sprinkle with the onion, bay leaf, parsley and juniper berries. Pour on the wine, cover and marinate in the refrigerator for 3–4 hours or overnight, turning the escalopes occasionally.

2. Remove the escalopes from the marinade, reserving the marinade. Heat the butter and oil in a large frying pan and fry the escalopes for 3–4 minutes on each side. Transfer to a warmed serving dish and keep warm while making the sauce.

3. Strain the reserved marinade into the frying pan and stir to loosen any sediment. Increase the heat and boil rapidly for 3–4 minutes, until reduced. Stir in the redcurrant jelly and season the mixture to taste. Cook for 1–2 minutes, stirring, then pour over the escalopes. Serve immediately.

Venison Stew

Venison is becoming more widely available with the development of deer farming, and can be bought all year round thanks to freezing techniques. The rich gamey flavour of venison comes out well in this slow-cooked dish.

SERVES 4

700 g (1$\frac{1}{2}$ lb) shoulder of venison, cut into 1 cm ($\frac{1}{2}$ inch) cubes

50 g (2 oz) plain flour

salt and freshly ground pepper

25 g (1 oz) butter

15 ml (1 tbsp) vegetable oil

2 medium onions, skinned and chopped

2 carrots, sliced

300 ml ($\frac{1}{2}$ pint) beef stock

150 ml ($\frac{1}{4}$ pint) dry red wine

bouquet garni

10 ml (2 tsp) red wine vinegar

1. Toss the venison in the flour seasoned with salt and pepper, shaking off any excess. Heat the butter and the oil in a large frying pan and fry the meat for about 10 minutes or until well browned on all sides. Using a slotted spoon, transfer to an ovenproof casserole.

2. Fry the vegetables in the fat remaining in the frying pan until golden. Drain well and add to the meat in the casserole. Stir the rest of the flour into the fat in the pan and cook gently, stirring, until brown. Remove the pan from the heat and gradually stir in the stock and wine. Bring to the boil, stirring, until thickened.

3. Pour the sauce over the venison and season to taste, then add the bouquet garni and the vinegar.

4. Cover the casserole and cook at 170°C (325°F) mark 3 for about 2 hours or until the meat is tender. Remove the bouquet garni before serving.

Right: Pheasant with chestnuts (page 76)

Pheasant with Chestnuts

Many supermarkets now sell oven-ready fresh or frozen pheasant during the season. You may also be able to buy fresh game from your butcher, in which case ask for the bird to be plucked and drawn. The tender flesh is deliciously contrasted with crunchy chestnuts in this richly flavoured dish.

SERVES 4

25 g (1 oz) butter
15 ml (1 tbsp) vegetable oil
2 oven-ready pheasants, jointed
2 medium onions, skinned and sliced
225 g (8 oz) peeled chestnuts
45 ml (3 tbsp) plain wholemeal flour
450 ml ($\frac{3}{4}$ pint) chicken stock
150 ml ($\frac{1}{4}$ pint) dry red wine
salt and freshly ground pepper
grated rind and juice of $\frac{1}{2}$ orange
10 ml (2 tsp) redcurrant jelly
bouquet garni

1. Heat the butter and oil in a large frying pan and fry the pheasant joints for about 5 minutes or until browned. Remove from the pan and put into an ovenproof casserole.

2. Fry the onions and chestnuts in the oil and butter remaining in the pan for a few minutes or until brown, then add to the pheasant.

3. Stir the flour into the fat in the pan and cook, stirring, for 2–3 minutes. Remove from the heat and gradually stir in the stock and wine. Bring to the boil, stirring continuously, until thickened and smooth. Season to taste and pour over the pheasant in the casserole. Add the orange rind and juice, redcurrant jelly and bouquet garni.

4. Cover the casserole and bake at 180°C (350°F) mark 4 for about 1 hour or until the pheasant is tender. Remove the bouquet garni before serving.

Duck with Cumberland Sauce

The rich flesh of wild duck is admirably partnered by the sweet sharp flavour of Cumberland sauce.

SERVES 4

4 duckling portions
salt and freshly ground pepper
finely shredded rind and juice of 1 large orange
finely shredded rind and juice of 1 lemon
60 ml (4 tbsp) redcurrant jelly
10 ml (2 tsp) cornflour
60 ml (4 tbsp) port
30 ml (2 tbsp) brandy
fresh lemon balm sprigs, to garnish

1. Prick the duckling portions all over with a sharp skewer or fork, then sprinkle with salt and pepper.

2. Place the duckling portions on a wire rack over a roasting tin. Roast at 190°C (375°F) mark 5 for 45–60 minutes or until the skin is crisp and the juices run clear when the thickest parts of the duckling portions are pricked with a skewer.

3. Meanwhile, make the sauce. Put the orange and lemon juices into a small saucepan, add the shreds of orange and lemon rind, cover and simmer gently for 5 minutes.

4. Add the redcurrant jelly and let it melt slowly over a gentle heat. Mix the cornflour with the port, then stir into the sauce and bring to the boil, stirring until the sauce thickens.

5. When the duckling portions are cooked, put them on a warmed serving dish and keep hot while the sauce is finished. Pour off the fat from the roasting tin, leaving the cooking juices behind, then add the brandy and stir over a gentle heat, scraping up the sediment from the bottom of the tin.

6. Add the sauce, stir well and serve with the duckling. Garnish with lemon balm.

Partridges 'Stewed' with Red Wine and Anchovies

Anchovies used to be used quite frequently in meat, poultry and game dishes to enhance and enrich the dish without being allowed to dominate the other flavours. Cooked in this way, older partridges—or other game birds, pigeon, hare or venison—become deliciously tender. The dish should traditionally be served with butter beans and Brussels sprouts.

SERVES 4–6

1 onion, skinned and finely chopped

white part of 1 long thin leek, finely chopped

1 small carrot, finely chopped

bouquet garni of 4 parsley sprigs, sprig of lovage, sprig of thyme and a small sprig of sage

2 partridges

450 ml ($\frac{3}{4}$ pint) game stock

2 anchovy fillets

50 g (2 oz) unsalted butter

450 ml ($\frac{3}{4}$ pint) claret or similar red wine

salt and freshly ground pepper

croûtons dipped in chopped parsley, to garnish

1. Mix the vegetables together in a heavy flameproof casserole. Add the bouquet garni and partridges. Pour in the stock and bring to simmering point. Cover with foil and a lid and cook gently for about 1 hour.

2. Pound the anchovies with half the butter, then add to the casserole with the claret and seasoning. Bring to simmering point again, then re-cover with the foil and lid and cook for a further 1$\frac{1}{2}$ hours.

3. Transfer the partridges to a warmed serving plate and keep warm. Discard the bouquet garni and boil the liquid until reduced and slightly thickened. Pass through a sieve, if wished and reheat over a low heat. Stir in the remaining butter, taste and adjust the seasoning.

4. Pour the sauce over the partridges. Garnish with the croûtons and serve.

Pigeons in a Pot with Plums

Fruit is widely used in savoury recipes and the delicate, slightly sharp flavour of plums goes well with game. Pigeons are available in early autumn, when plums are at their best.

SERVES 4

25 g (1 oz) butter

15 ml (1 tbsp) vegetable oil

4 young pigeons, prepared

10 ml (2 tsp) plain wholemeal flour

1 medium onion, skinned and chopped

2 cloves

15 ml (1 tbsp) chopped fresh mixed herbs, such as rosemary, sage, thyme, or 5 ml (1 tsp) dried mixed herbs

100 ml (4 fl oz) port

450 g (1 lb) purple plums, stoned and halved

salt and freshly ground pepper

freshly grated nutmeg

1. Heat the butter and oil in a large frying pan. Coat the pigeons lightly in the flour, shaking off any excess, then add to the pan and fry, turning occasionally, until lightly browned on all sides. Transfer to an ovenproof casserole.

2. Stir the onion into the frying pan and fry gently until beginning to soften. Spoon over the pigeons, then sprinkle the cloves and herbs over the top.

3. Stir the port into the frying pan, bring to the boil, then pour over the pigeons. Arrange the plums over the top. Cover tightly and bake at 170°C (325°F) mark 3 for 1$\frac{1}{2}$ hours or until the pigeons are tender.

4. Transfer the pigeons and plums to a warmed serving platter. Boil the juices for 2–3 minutes to thicken them and concentrate the flavour. Season to taste with salt, pepper and nutmeg, then pour over the pigeons. Serve at once.

SUMMER BUFFET FOR 15–20

Slices of Beef in Wine Jelly

These savoury beef jellies can be made entirely the day before the party, and kept in the refrigerator. Depending on the weather, unmould 1–2 hours before serving; if the weather is very hot, leave the unmoulding until as late as possible.

45 ml (3 tbsp) oil

4 fillets of beef, each weighing about 400 g (14 oz), tied into neat cylindrical shapes

750 ml (1¼ pints) lightly jellied veal stock

350 ml (12 fl oz) medium-bodied red wine

350 ml (12 fl oz) sercial (dry) Madeira

2 small bay leaves, torn in half

fresh parsley sprig

small fresh rosemary sprig

12.5 ml (2½ tsp) gelatine

45 ml (3 tbsp) green peppercorns

curly endive and fresh herb leaves or small sprigs, to garnish

1. Heat the oil in a roasting tin on top of the cooker, add the fillets and sear evenly all over. Transfer to the oven and roast at 220°C (425°F) mark 7 for 10 minutes (the beef will be rare).

2. Using tongs or a fish slice, transfer the fillets to a cooling rack with a baking tray placed underneath. Leave to cool completely. When cold, cut the beef into 1–2 cm (½–¾ inch) thick slices.

3. Boil the stock, wine and Madeira with the herbs until reduced by half.

4. Dissolve the gelatine in 25 ml (1½ tbsp) water in a bowl placed over a saucepan of hot water. Remove the bowl from the saucepan. Remove the herbs from the reduced liquor and slowly stir the liquor into the gelatine.

5. Spoon a thin layer of this aspic over the bottom of ramekins or other similar small dishes, one for each slice of beef. Chill until set. Keep the remaining aspic liquid at room temperature.

6. Place about 2.5 ml (½ tsp) green peppercorns in the centre of each dish on the layer of aspic. Carefully place a slice of beef on top. Spoon in sufficient aspic to surround and just cover each slice. Chill until set.

7. Arrange a bed of finely shredded curly endive on cold plates. Unmould the beef jellies on to the plates and garnish with leaves or small sprigs of fresh herbs.

Left: Duck with Cumberland sauce (page 76)

Chicken Breasts in Muscat Wine with Apricots

For convenience, start this recipe two days before the party. Finish off the dish the day before the party and keep it in the refrigerator overnight. If you do not have a casserole large enough, use two or three.

2 bottles of dry Alsatian muscat wine

3 large shallots, skinned and finely chopped

about 8 fresh thyme sprigs

2 bay leaves, torn in half

15 ml (1 tbsp) finely chopped lemon rind

salt and freshly ground pepper

20 chicken breasts (on the bone)

150 g (5 oz) sugar

2 cinnamon sticks

1.8 kg (4 lb) ripe apricots, halved and stoned

fresh chervil sprigs, to garnish

1. Pour 900 ml (1½ pints) of the wine into a large casserole, bring to the boil and boil rapidly until reduced to 75 ml (3 fl oz). Pour in the remaining wine and add the shallots, herbs, lemon rind and seasoning.

2. Add the chicken breasts, skin side down. Bring just to boiling point, then cover tightly and transfer to the oven. Cook at 170°C (325°F) mark 3 for 45–50 minutes, turning the chicken over after 20 minutes and then again after a further 20 minutes. Leave the chicken to cool in the liquor.

3. Drain the chicken, reserving the liquor. Discard the skin, and remove the breasts from the bones in one piece. Remove any fat from the surface of the liquor. Return the breasts to the liquor, cover and refrigerate overnight.

4. The next day, the liquor should have gelled slightly. Remove any remaining fat from the surface. Lift out the chicken breasts and set aside. Warm the liquor slightly, then pour it through a sieve lined with a piece of muslin or cheesecloth.

5. Reserve about 150 ml (¼ pint) of the liquor and put the remainder in a saucepan. Add the sugar. Heat, stirring, until the sugar has dissolved, then add the cinnamon sticks and bring to the boil.

6. Lower the heat and add about one-third of the apricots. They should be covered by the liquor. Poach the fruit for about 5 minutes. Transfer to a bowl using a slotted spoon. Poach the remaining apricots in the same way and add to the bowl.

7. Pour the liquor over the apricots and leave to cool, moving the apricots around from time to time so that they are equally soaked. Cover and chill.

8. Carve the chicken breasts into thin slices. Arrange the slices in fan shapes on one or two large, cold platters. Brush the slices lightly with the reserved liquor.

9. Remove the apricots from their liquor, using a slotted spoon, and arrange them on and around the chicken, cutting some of the apricot halves in half again. Garnish the platter with sprigs of chervil.

Sole and Smoked Salmon Terrine

This terrine will serve 8–10 people, so make two. This terrine looks most attractive, with its creamy white exterior, its pale pink layer, and core of dark green spinach purée. Make the day before and refrigerate until required.

550 g (1¼ lb) Dover sole fillets, skinned

15 ml (1 tbsp) lemon juice

salt and white pepper

2 egg whites

150 ml (¼ pint) double cream

175 g (6 oz) young spinach leaves, shredded

FOR THE SMOKED SALMON CREAM

175 g (6 oz) smoked salmon

lemon juice

1 egg white, size 6

75 ml (3 fl oz) crème fraîche or double cream

cayenne pepper

FOR THE GARNISH

red and green peppers, thinly pared cucumber skin and lemon rind

1. Put the sole in a blender or food processor and blend to a purée. Add the lemon juice and salt and then the egg whites. For a really smooth terrine, pass the mixture through a fine sieve.

2. Return the purée to the blender or food processor and, with the motor running, very gradually pour in the cream. Season with pepper. Chill for at least 1 hour.

3. Put the smoked salmon in a blender or food processor and blend to a purée. Add a squeeze of lemon juice and then the egg white. Pass through a fine sieve as for the sole, then return to the blender or food processor. With the motor running, gradually pour in the crème fraîche or cream. Season with cayenne pepper. Chill for about 1 hour.

4. Cook the spinach with 15 ml (1 tbsp) water until wilted. Drain well, then rinse in cold running water. Drain well again, pressing down on the spinach to extract as much water as possible. Purée in a blender or food processor and season.

5. For the garnish, grill the peppers until they are soft and the skins are charred all over. Allow to cool, then peel the peppers. Remove the cores and seeds. Cut the peppers into decorative shapes. Arrange the pepper shapes, cucumber skin and lemon rind on the bottom of a lightly oiled 25 × 10 cm (10 × 4 inch) terrine.

6. Carefully cover the bottom and sides of the terrine with about two-thirds of the sole mixture. Leave an open channel in the centre.

7. Place about half of the smoked salmon mixture in the channel, then cover the salmon with the spinach purée. Cover with the remaining smoked salmon mixture and cover this with the remaining sole mixture. Cover the terrine with greased greaseproof paper.

8. Put the terrine into a roasting tin. Surround with boiling water and bake at 170°C (325°F) mark 3 for about 50 minutes or until just set in the centre. Remove the terrine from the oven and leave to cool. Drain off any excess cooking liquid.

9. Carefully unmould the terrine on to a cold plate. Garnish the plate with thinly pared strips of cucumber skin.

Overleaf: Tomato and mange-tout salad (page 84), sole and smoked salmon terrine (above), avocado, orange and cucumber salad (page 85)

Tomato and Mange-tout Salad

This salad has an attractive contrast in both colour and texture. The mange-tout can be cooked and the dressing made the day before. Assemble the salad on the morning of the party.

450 g (1 lb) mange-tout, preferably very small ones

30 ml (2 tbsp) red wine vinegar

3 garlic cloves, skinned and crushed

5 ml (1 tsp) Dijon mustard

salt and freshly ground pepper

90 ml (6 tbsp) olive oil

30 ml (2 tbsp) chopped fresh parsley

45 ml (3 tbsp) chopped fresh basil

900 g (2 lb) ripe but firm tomatoes, sliced

1. String the mange-tout, if necessary. Blanch them in boiling salted water for 2 minutes, then pour them into a large colander and refresh under a cold tap. Drain very well and dry very thoroughly on clean tea-towels. If the mange-tout are large, cut them into slices, cutting on a slant. Leave small ones whole.

2. Put the vinegar, garlic, mustard and seasoning into a mixing bowl and stir well until the salt dissolves. Whisk in the olive oil. Stir in the parsley and basil.

3. Arrange the tomato slices and mange-tout in attractive layers on a large serving dish, spooning the dressing over each layer.

Curried New Potato Salad

This salad can be made entirely a day, or even two days, before the party, but add the parsley garnish at the last minute. Keep the salad in its serving bowl, covered, in the refrigerator. Remove 1–2 hours before serving.

2.3 kg (5 lb) small new potatoes

25 ml (5 tsp) white wine vinegar

5 ml (1 tsp) mustard powder

3 garlic cloves, skinned and crushed

salt and freshly ground pepper

90 ml (6 tbsp) olive oil

900 ml (1½ pints) mayonnaise

45 ml (3 tbsp) mild curry powder

chopped fresh parsley, to garnish

1. Cook the potatoes in boiling salted water until they are just tender. Drain well and allow to cool. Cut larger potatoes into thick slices.

2. Put the vinegar into a large mixing bowl with the mustard, garlic and seasoning and stir until the salt dissolves. Whisk in the olive oil. Add the cooled potatoes to the dressing and mix together gently until the potatoes are well coated with the dressing.

3. Mix the mayonnaise and curry powder together. Pour over the potatoes and carefully fold together.

4. Spoon the salad into a large serving bowl, cover and refrigerate until ready to serve sprinkled with parsley.

Mixed Lettuce Salad

For this salad, three kinds of lettuce are dressed with a mixture of cream, Meaux mustard and lemon juice. Almonds add a subtle crunch. The dressing can be made one or two days ahead, and stored in a screw-topped jar in the refrigerator. The lettuces can be washed and shredded the evening before, and kept in a polythene bag in the refrigerator. Toss with the dressing just before serving.

1 Webb's Wonder or iceberg lettuce, shredded
1 medium Cos lettuce, shredded
1 round lettuce, shredded
40 g (1½ oz) flaked almonds, half lightly toasted

FOR THE DRESSING
325 ml (11 fl oz) single cream
30 ml (2 tbsp) Meaux mustard
100 ml (4 fl oz) lemon juice
salt and freshly ground pepper

1. Blend the single cream into the mustard, then add the lemon juice and seasoning. Cover and keep cool.
2. Toss the lettuces together and put into one or two cold salad bowls.
3. Stir the dressing and pour over the lettuces. Toss lightly, then sprinkle the nuts over. Toss again very briefly and serve at once.

Avocado, Orange and Cucumber Salad

This is a most decorative salad, with the cardamom giving an unexpected and delicious flavour. The cucumber and orange can be prepared well in advance, but not the avocado as it will tend to discolour if it is left to stand too long.

2 large cucumbers
salt and freshly ground pepper
5 oranges
4 large ripe but firm avocados
15 ml (1 tbsp) white wine vinegar
5 ml (1 tsp) freshly ground cardamom
45 ml (3 tbsp) olive oil
grated orange rind, to garnish

1. Peel the cucumbers, cut each one in half lengthways and scoop out the seeds. Cut the cucumbers crossways into 0.5 cm (¼ inch) thick slices. Put the slices into a mixing bowl and sprinkle lightly with salt, then cover and leave to stand for 1 hour (the salt extracts the excess water and crisps the cucumber).
2. Meanwhile, peel the oranges and cut them into segments, cutting between the connective tissue. Squeeze the remaining tissue over a bowl, to extract the juice. Cut the segments into smaller pieces and add them to the juice.
3. Cut each avocado in half and remove the stone, then carefully pull away the skin from each half. Cut the avocados crossways into slices.
4. Thoroughly rinse and drain the cucumber on absorbent kitchen paper.
5. Put the vinegar, cardamom and seasoning in a salad bowl and stir well until the salt dissolves. Whisk in the olive oil. Add the oranges, orange juice, avocados and cucumber to the dressing, and mix gently together. Garnish with grated orange rind.

Overleaf: Chicken and broccoli pie (page 66), platter of steamed baby vegetables (page 97)

Sorrel and Lettuce Mayonnaise

This sauce has a delicate flavour, and is a beautiful pale green colour. It can be made in advance.

100 g (4 oz) Webb's Wonder or iceberg lettuce, shredded

100 g (4 oz) small sorrel leaves, shredded

salt and freshly ground pepper

1 egg, at room temperature

2.5 ml ($\frac{1}{2}$ tsp) mustard powder

lemon juice

300 ml ($\frac{1}{2}$ pint) olive oil

1. Cook the lettuce and sorrel with 45 ml (3 tbsp) water for about 4 minutes or until the sorrel has 'fallen'. The lettuce will remain quite crisp. Drain well, season and cool.

2. Blend the egg with the mustard powder and lemon juice in a blender or food processor. With the motor running, pour in the oil in a slow steady stream. Transfer to a bowl and season. Fold in the sorrel and lettuce.

Geranium Cream with Red Summer Fruits

This rich cream, which is a mixture of double cream and cream cheese, is delicately scented with geranium leaves. The red summer fruits served with it — a combination of raspberries, strawberries (wild if possible) and redcurrants — look beautiful, with their jewel-like colours surrounding the white cream.

300 ml ($\frac{1}{2}$ pint) double cream

6 sweet geranium leaves, bruised

900 g (2 lb) cream cheese

175 g (6 oz) caster sugar, or to taste

1.4 kg (3 lb) red summer fruits, such as raspberries, small strawberries and redcurrants, chilled

caster sugar, to serve

1. Gently heat the cream with the geranium leaves in the top of a double boiler, or in a bowl placed over a saucepan of hot water, for 10–15 minutes or until it just reaches simmering point. Do not allow to boil. Remove from the heat, cover and leave to cool.

2. Strain the cream, then gradually stir it into the cheese, stirring until smooth. Rinse the geranium leaves, dry them and stir into the cream mixture. Cover and leave in a cool place for 12 hours.

3. Remove the geranium leaves and stir in sugar to taste. Spoon the cream into a mound on a cold decorative plate. Spoon the fruits around. Serve sugar for sprinkling over the fruits separately.

Passion Fruit Gâteau

This layered cake, with its exotic passion fruit
filling, will serve 8–10, so for 15–20 guests, make
two cakes. If you like, you can make the cakes well
in advance and freeze them, then on the day of the
party you just need to thaw, fill and ice them and
decorate with pistachio nuts.
MAKES ONE 23 cm (9 inch) CAKE

4 eggs, separated
100 g (4 oz) caster sugar
100 g (4 oz) self-raising flour
pinch of salt
25 g (1 oz) unsalted butter, melted

FOR THE PASSION FRUIT CREAM
350 g (12 oz) fromage blanc
75 ml (5 tbsp) thick natural yogurt
few drops of orange-flower water
25 ml (1½ tbsp) icing sugar
5 ripe passion fruit, halved

FOR THE DECORATION
150 ml (¼ pint) double cream, lightly whipped
75–100 g (3–4 oz) shelled pistachio nuts, chopped
shelled whole pistachio nuts

1. Whisk the egg yolks and sugar together until thick and pale. Sift the flour and salt over and fold in lightly. Whisk the egg whites until stiff but not dry, then lightly fold into the yolk mixture. Trickle the butter over and carefully fold in.

2. Turn the mixture into a greased and base-lined 23 cm (9 inch) loose-bottomed cake tin. Bake at 180°C (350°F) mark 4 for 25–35 minutes or until risen and springy to the touch when lightly pressed in the centre.

3. Leave to cool slightly in the tin, then turn out on to a wire rack covered with a tea-towel. Remove the lining paper and leave to cool completely.

4. For the passion fruit cream, mix the fromage blanc, yogurt, orange-flower water and icing sugar together. Stir in the passion fruit flesh.

5. Cut the cake into three equal layers. Spread about one-third of the passion fruit cream over the bottom layer. Place the second layer gently on top and cover with another one-third of the passion fruit cream, not taking it right to the edge. Spread the remaining passion fruit cream over the top cake layer, not taking it right to the edge, and gently place this on top of the cake.

6. Reserving a little of the whipped cream for piping around the top of the cake, spread the remainder over the sides of the cake. Coat the sides with chopped pistachio nuts.

7. Spoon the reserved cream into a piping bag fitted with a small star nozzle and pipe a border around the top edge of the cake. Decorate with the pistachio nuts.

ACCOMPANIMENTS

Baked Courgettes with Mushrooms

This creamy combination of courgettes and mushrooms is ideal for serving with grilled meats.

SERVES 6

50 g (2 oz) butter

1.1 kg (2½ lb) courgettes, trimmed and cut into 0.5 cm (¼ inch) slices

salt and freshly ground pepper

225 g (8 oz) button mushrooms, wiped and sliced

150 ml (¼ pint) soured cream

chopped fresh parsley, to garnish

1. Melt the butter in a medium roasting tin, add the courgettes and turn over in the butter. Season well. Roast in the oven at 200°C (400°F) mark 6 for 20 minutes.

2. Stir the sliced mushrooms into the courgettes and return to the oven for a further 10–15 minutes.

3. Stir the soured cream and then mix through the vegetables. Heat on top of the cooker until bubbling, then taste and adjust the seasoning. Spoon the vegetables into a serving dish and serve hot, garnished with parsley.

Leek Mousses

Delicious and impressive looking, these pale green mousses go well with fish dishes, or can be served on their own as a starter or light lunch dish.

MAKES 8

450 g (1 lb) leeks, trimmed, thinly sliced and washed

25 g (1 oz) butter

30 ml (2 tbsp) plain wholemeal flour

300 ml (½ pint) milk

150 g (5 oz) soft cheese with garlic and herbs

2 eggs

25 g (1 oz) fresh wholemeal breadcrumbs

salt and freshly ground pepper

1. Place the leeks in a medium saucepan of boiling salted water and cook for about 5 minutes or until tender. Drain well and rinse with cold water.

2. Meanwhile, put the butter, flour and milk in a medium saucepan. Heat, whisking continuously, until the sauce thickens, boils and is smooth. Simmer for 2–3 minutes. Add half the cooked leeks and leave to cool.

3. Place the cooled sauce, soft cheese, eggs and breadcrumbs in a blender or food processor and blend until almost smooth. Season to taste.

4. Lightly grease eight 100 ml (4 fl oz) ramekin dishes and scatter a few of the reserved leeks in the bottom of each. Carefully pour the sauce on top of the leeks.

5. Place the ramekins in a roasting tin. Add enough hot water to come halfway up the sides of the dishes. Cover the roasting tin tightly with foil.

6. Bake at 180°C (350°F) mark 4 for about 1 hour or until just firm to the touch. Stand for 4–5 minutes before serving.

Left: Baked courgettes with mushrooms (above), leek mousses (above)

Creamed Carrot and Parsnip

This interesting combination of mashed vegetables
makes a change from mashed potatoes.
SERVES 6

900 g (2 lb) carrots, peeled and cubed
450 g (1 lb) parsnips, peeled and cut into small pieces
50 g (2 oz) butter
salt and freshly ground pepper
pinch of grated nutmeg
chopped fresh parsley, to garnish

1. Cook the carrots and parsnips together in boiling salted water for about 25 minutes or until tender. Drain well and mash, using a potato masher.
2. Return to the pan with the butter, seasoning and nutmeg and cook over a high heat, stirring frequently, to drive off any moisture.
3. Beat well to mix the vegetables and pile into a warm serving dish. Garnish with chopped fresh parsley to serve.

Carrots with Mint and Lemon

Tender young carrots, in the shops during spring and
early summer, have a lovely sweet flavour which is
brought out to the full by the sugar and lemon juice
in this recipe. Unwashed carrots, which sometimes
still have their feathery foliage, keep better than
those sold washed and pre-packed.
SERVES 4

700 g (1½ lb) small new carrots, trimmed and scrubbed
salt and freshly ground pepper
finely grated rind and juice of ½ lemon
5 ml (1 tsp) light soft brown sugar
15 g (½ oz) butter
30 ml (2 tbsp) chopped fresh mint

1. Cook the carrots in boiling salted water for about 10 minutes or until just tender. Drain.
2. Return the carrots to the pan with the remaining ingredients and toss together over a high heat until the butter melts. Serve at once.

Julienned Courgettes in Garlic Butter

Strongly flavoured with garlic, this dish makes a
particularly good accompaniment for lamb.
SERVES 12

1.8 kg (4 lb) courgettes
100 g (4 oz) butter
2 large garlic cloves, skinned and crushed
salt and freshly ground pepper

1. Cut the courgettes into fine shreds in a mouli-julienne, using the medium-sized disc. Alternatively, grate them coarsely.
2. Put the shreds into a large colander and leave to drain for about 1 hour. During this time the excess liquid will drain away from the courgettes.
3. Melt the butter in two large frying pans and add the garlic. Divide the courgettes evenly between the two pans and season well with salt and pepper. Cook the courgettes gently for about 20–25 minutes or until they are just tender but still retain their shape. Do not allow to brown or to overcook. Spoon the courgettes into a large warmed serving dish.

Kohlrabi with Cream Sauce

Cooked in cream, kohlrabi is a tasty dish to serve with meat, fish or poultry.

SERVES 4

4 small kohlrabi, trimmed
30 ml (2 tbsp) finely chopped shallots
175 ml (6 fl oz) dry white wine
150 ml ($\frac{1}{4}$ pint) double cream
25 g (1 oz) butter, diced
5 ml (1 tsp) lemon juice
salt and freshly ground pepper
parsley sprigs, to garnish

1. Place the kohlrabi in the top part of a steamer or in a colander, cover and cook over simmering water for about 30 minutes or until tender.

2. Meanwhile, simmer the shallots in the wine in a covered pan for 5 minutes or until tender. Bring to the boil and boil until the wine has reduced to 45 ml (3 tbsp). Stir in the cream and simmer until slightly thickened.

3. Press the sauce through a sieve, return it to the rinsed-out pan and reheat gently. Gradually whisk in the butter, one piece at a time. Stir in the lemon juice. Season and keep warm. Do not allow the sauce to boil or it will curdle.

4. Remove the kohlrabi from the heat, cool slightly, then rub off the skin. Slice finely and arrange the slices in a warmed serving dish. Spoon over the sauce and garnish with the parsley sprigs.

Spinach with Nutmeg

Spinach is one of the most flavoursome vegetables. A coating of melted butter and some freshly grated nutmeg help make the most of it.

SERVES 6

1.8 kg (4 lb) fresh spinach
salt and freshly ground pepper
50 g (2 oz) butter
large pinch of freshly grated nutmeg

1. Trim the spinach, removing any coarse stalks and brown or damaged leaves. Wash well in several changes of cold water, making sure all the grit is removed. Drain in a colander.

2. Place the minimum of water—1 cm ($\frac{1}{2}$ inch) is ample—in the bases of one or two large saucepans. Add the spinach and season generously.

3. Cover tightly and cook over a moderate heat for about 10 minutes or until tender. Push down and turn the spinach over once or twice during cooking.

4. Drain in a colander and press firmly with a potato masher to extract all moisture. Chop roughly.

5. Melt the butter in a medium saucepan, add the spinach with plenty of seasoning and cook over a moderate heat, stirring occasionally, until piping hot.

6. Add a generous grating of nutmeg and spoon into a serving dish.

Overleaf: Sliced potatoes with parsley and celery seeds (page 97), roast pork with apples (page 52)

Runner Beans with Onions and Tomatoes

Runner beans used to be grown for their attractive red flowers and have only been produced for food since the last century.

SERVES 4–6

15 g (½ oz) butter

1 medium onion, skinned and chopped

1 garlic clove, skinned and crushed

397 g (14 oz) can chopped tomatoes

700 g (1½ lb) young runner beans, topped and tailed and cut into 1 cm (½ inch) lengths

15 ml (1 tbsp) chopped fresh basil or 5 ml (1 tsp) dried basil

salt and freshly ground pepper

1. Melt the butter in a large saucepan and cook the onion and garlic gently for 3–5 minutes or until softened but not browned. Add the tomatoes with their juice, bring to the boil and simmer for 10–15 minutes or until reduced.

2. Stir the beans into the sauce with the dried basil, if using, cover tightly and cook for 10–15 minutes or until the beans are tender but still crisp. Stir in the fresh basil, if using, and season to taste. Serve hot or cold.

Onions à la Grecque

This recipe can be served as an accompaniment to boiled ham or roasted meat or poultry.

SERVES 8

900 g (2 lb) small pickling onions

75 ml (5 tbsp) olive oil

5 ml (1 tsp) sugar

150 ml (¼ pint) dry white wine

10 ml (2 tsp) tomato purée

salt and freshly ground pepper

30 ml (2 tbsp) chopped fresh parsley

1. Blanch the onions in boiling water for 1 minute only, then drain and rinse under cold running water. Remove the onion skins.

2. Put the onions in a large, heavy-based pan with 300 ml (½ pint) water and the remaining ingredients, except the chopped parsley. Add salt and pepper to taste. Bring to the boil, then lower the heat, cover and simmer gently for 30 minutes.

3. Uncover and cook for a further 15 minutes or until the onions are tender. Taste and adjust the seasoning, then stir in the chopped parsley. Turn into a warmed serving dish and serve hot.

Celeriac Purée

The purée can be prepared in advance and kept covered in the refrigerator. To serve, place the purée in a bowl over a saucepan of hot water and reheat, stirring frequently.

SERVES 6

900 g (2 lb) celeriac, peeled and chopped

450 ml (¾ pint) milk

40 g (1½ oz) unsalted butter

40 ml (1½ fl oz) double cream

salt and white pepper

1. Cook the celeriac in simmering salted milk for 6 minutes or until tender. Drain the celeriac well, reserving the milk. Purée the celeriac in a blender or food processor.

2. Heat the butter in a non-stick saucepan and stir in the celeriac purée, then heat, stirring constantly, to drive off excess moisture.

3. Beat in the cream and enough of the reserved milk to give a creamy consistency. Add seasoning to taste.

Sliced Potatoes with Parsley and Celery Seeds

The simple addition of fresh parsley and celery seeds makes all the difference to a dish of sliced boiled potatoes.

SERVES 8

1.4 kg (3 lb) medium potatoes
50 g (2 oz) butter
10 ml (2 tsp) celery seeds
45 ml (3 tbsp) chopped fresh parsley
salt and freshly ground pepper

1. Scrub the potatoes. Cover with cold salted water and bring to the boil. Boil for about 30 minutes or until tender.

2. Drain well, then cut the potatoes into 0.5 cm ($\frac{1}{4}$ inch) slices and place in a shallow serving dish.

3. Melt the butter in a pan, add the celery seeds, parsley and plenty of seasoning and spoon over the potatoes. Serve hot.

Platter of Steamed Baby Vegetables

You can use any tiny, new vegetables you like for this attractive platter. Serve with melted butter flavoured with finely chopped parsley and chives, if you like.

SERVES 6–8

12 small young carrots with tops, scrubbed
12 small courgettes, about 2.5 cm (1 inch) in diameter
12 baby turnips with tops, scrubbed
350 g (12 oz) shelled young broad beans
350 g (12 oz) French beans, cut into 5 cm (2 inch) lengths
melted unsalted butter, for serving

1. Trim the carrots down to small neat shapes, leaving the tops intact. Cut and trim the courgettes until they resemble torpedo shapes, leaving the skin on. Trim the turnips, leaving the tops on.

2. Place the carrots in the top part of a steamer and place over boiling water. Cover and cook for 1 minute. Add the turnips and broad beans and cook for 30 seconds. Add the French beans and cook for $1\frac{1}{2}$ minutes. Add the courgettes and cook for a final 2 minutes.

3. Squeeze the broad beans gently between the thumb and first finger so that the tender centres pop out.

4. Arrange the vegetables on one large or six small plates. Serve with melted butter.

Overleaf: Frozen passion fruit soufflé (page 105), gravad lax (page 25)

Cauliflower and Potato Bake

Cauliflower is often eaten with a rich creamy sauce, as in this recipe. Freshly grated nutmeg and garlic add flavour to the sauce, which is soaked up deliciously by the potatoes.

SERVES 4

450 g (1 lb) new potatoes, thinly sliced

1 small cauliflower, broken into florets

1 garlic clove, skinned and crushed

pinch of freshly grated nutmeg

150 ml ($\frac{1}{4}$ pint) single cream or buttermilk

50 g (2 oz) Cheddar cheese, grated

1. Cook the potatoes in boiling salted water for 5 minutes. Drain well.

2. Layer the potatoes and cauliflower in a lightly buttered 1.1 litre (2 pint) ovenproof serving dish. Stir the garlic and nutmeg into the cream and pour over the vegetables.

3. Sprinkle with the cheese, cover and bake at 180°C (350°F) mark 4 for 45–50 minutes or until the vegetables are tender. Uncover and place under a medium grill until lightly browned. Serve at once, straight from the dish.

Pumpkin Gratin

Pumpkins are easily obtainable and are a familiar sight in shops in autumn. They have come to be associated with Hallowe'en, and pumpkin pie is a traditional Thanksgiving Day dish in America.

SERVES 6

45 ml (3 tbsp) olive oil

1 large onion, thinly sliced

900 g (2 lb) pumpkin, peeled, seeded and cut into small chunks

10 ml (2 tsp) chopped fresh thyme

salt and freshly ground pepper

25 g (1 oz) Parmesan cheese, grated

1. Heat 30 ml (2 tbsp) oil in a pan, add the onion and fry for about 10 minutes or until softened and lightly browned.

2. Meanwhile, parboil the pumpkin in salted water for 10 minutes. Drain, reserving 45 ml (3 tbsp) of the cooking liquid. Mix the pumpkin with the reserved liquid, the thyme, remaining oil and seasoning.

3. Spread the onion over the bottom of a gratin dish. Put the pumpkin on top. Bake at 190°C (375°F) mark 5 for 30 minutes. Sprinkle with the Parmesan and bake for 15 minutes longer.

Desserts

Raspberry and Walnut Shortbread

This is a truly mouth-watering dessert that tastes even better than it looks. The walnuts are ground and added to the shortbread mixture for a subtle nutty flavour. The dessert could also be made with strawberries.

SERVES 8

100 g (4 oz) walnut pieces
100 g (4 oz) butter
75 g (3 oz) caster sugar
175 g (6 oz) plain flour
450 g (1 lb) fresh raspberries
50 g (2 oz) icing sugar
30 ml (2 tbsp) raspberry-flavoured liqueur or kirsch (optional)
300 ml ($\frac{1}{2}$ pint) whipping cream

1. Draw three 20.5 cm (8 inch) circles on sheets of non-stick baking paper. Place the paper sheets on baking sheets.
2. Grind the walnuts finely in a blender or food processor.
3. Cream the butter and sugar together in a mixing bowl until pale and fluffy, then beat in the walnuts and flour. Divide the dough into three shortbread portions.
4. Put a portion of shortbread dough in the centre of each parchment circle and press out with the heel of your hand until the dough is the same size as the circle.
5. Cut one of the circles into eight triangles with a sharp knife and ease them slightly apart. Refrigerate the circles and triangles for 30 minutes. Bake at 190°C (375°F) mark 5 for 15–20 minutes, swapping over the baking sheets halfway through to ensure the pastries brown evenly. Leave to cool and harden for 10 minutes on the paper, then transfer to wire racks to cool completely.
6. Meanwhile, reserve one-third of the raspberries for decoration. Put the rest in a bowl with the icing sugar and liqueur, if using. Crush the raspberries with a fork, then leave them to macerate while the shortbread rounds are cooling.
7. Assemble the dessert just before serving, to ensure that the shortbread remains crisp. Whip the cream until thick, then fold in the crushed raspberries and juice. Stand one round of pastry on a flat serving plate and spread with half of the cream mixture. Top with the remaining round of pastry, then the remaining cream mixture.
8. Arrange the triangles of pastry on top of the cream, wedging them in at an angle. Scatter the reserved whole raspberries in between. Serve as soon as possible.

Above: Hazelnut gâteau (page 105)
Right: Autumn pudding (page 104)

Champagne Syllabub

This is an ideal special-occasion dessert to serve at a dinner party or buffet.

SERVES 12

4 large lemons

1 large orange

450 ml ($\frac{3}{4}$ pint) Champagne

90 ml (6 tbsp) Grand Marnier

100 g (4 oz) caster sugar

900 ml (1$\frac{1}{2}$ pints) double cream

FOR THE DECORATION

thinly pared rind of 1 small orange

thinly pared rind of 1 small lemon

thinly pared rind of 1 lime

75 g (3 oz) granulated sugar

1. Very thinly pare the rind from the lemons and the orange, taking care not to remove any of the white pith. Squeeze the juice from the fruit and strain it.

2. Put the rinds and juice into a mixing bowl, then pour in the Champagne and Grand Marnier. Add the caster sugar and stir well until dissolved. Cover and leave to soak for 8 hours.

3. To make the decoration, cut the orange, lemon and lime rind into very fine shreds. Put the shreds into a saucepan with the sugar and 150 ml ($\frac{1}{4}$ pint) cold water.

4. Heat very gently until the sugar dissolves, then bring to the boil. Reduce the heat and cook gently until the shreds are very soft, and the sugar and water have reduced to a heavy syrup. Pour into a small bowl and cover. Chill.

5. Strain the Champagne liquid into a large, well-chilled mixing bowl. Discard the lemon and orange rinds. Pour the cream, in a thin stream, into the bowl, whisking all the time. Continue to whisk until the mixture thickens and retains its shape—take care not to over-whisk as the mixture will curdle.

6. Spoon the syllabub into twelve 200 ml (7 fl oz) serving glasses. Cover the tops of the glasses with cling film to prevent the syllabub from absorbing flavours from other foods that may be in the refrigerator. Refrigerate until ready to serve.

7. Just before serving, decorate each syllabub with the orange, lemon and lime shreds.

Autumn Pudding

Exactly the same as summer pudding, but this time the bread-lined basin is filled with a juicy mixture of the finest fruits of autumn.

SERVES 4–6

700 g (1$\frac{1}{2}$ lb) mixed autumn fruit, such as apples, blackberries and plums, prepared

about 25 g (1 oz) light soft brown sugar

8–10 thin slices of day-old bread, crusts removed

fresh fruit and mint sprigs, to decorate

1. Stew the fruit gently with 60–90 ml (4–6 tbsp) water and the sugar until soft but still retaining their shape.

2. Meanwhile, cut a round from one slice of bread to fit the bottom of a 1.1 litre (2 pint) pudding basin, and cut 6–8 slices of the bread into fingers about 5 cm (2 inches) wide. Put the round at the bottom of the basin and arrange the fingers overlapping around the sides.

3. When the fruit is cooked, and still hot, pour it gently into the basin, being careful not to disturb the bread framework. Reserve about 45 ml (3 tbsp) of the juice. When the basin is full, cut the remaining bread and use to cover the fruit so a lid is formed.

4. Cover with foil, then a plate or saucer which fits just inside the bowl and put a weight on top. Leave the pudding until cold, then put in the refrigerator and chill overnight.

5. To serve, run a knife carefully round the edge to loosen, then invert the pudding on to a serving dish. Pour the reserved juice over the top. Serve cold with cream. Decorate with fruit and mint sprigs.

Frozen Passion Fruit Soufflé

This velvety smooth soufflé will make the perfect ending to a dinner party. It should be made the day before.
SERVES 8

16 passion fruit
6 egg yolks
175 g (6 oz) caster sugar
600 ml (1 pint) double cream

1. Prepare a 1.1 litre (2 pint) soufflé dish by cutting a double strip of greaseproof paper long enough to fit around the dish, and wide enough to stand 5 cm (2 inches) above the rim. Secure the collar firmly around the dish.

2. Cut each passion fruit in half and scoop out the flesh and seeds into a nylon sieve placed over a small bowl. Press with a spoon to extract all of the juice—about 150 ml ($\frac{1}{4}$ pint).

3. Put the egg yolks into a large bowl and whisk well, preferably with an electric mixer, until very thick.

4. Put 60 ml (4 tbsp) of the passion fruit juice into a small saucepan with the caster sugar. Stir over a low heat until the sugar has dissolved, then bring to the boil and boil until the temperature reaches 110°C (230°F) on a sugar thermometer.

5. Whisk the syrup in a steady stream into the egg yolks, then continue whisking until the mixture cools and thickens. Gradually whisk in the remaining passion fruit juice, whisking until the mixture is thick and mousse-like.

6. Whip the cream until it just holds its shape. Fold the cream into the passion fruit mixture until no trace of white remains. Pour into the prepared soufflé dish, then freeze until firm. Once frozen, cover with cling film.

7. To serve, remove the soufflé from the freezer 20–30 minutes before serving and carefully peel off the cling film and paper.

Hazelnut Meringue Gâteau

This simple gâteau is perfect for the novice meringue-maker. The sharp flavour of the raspberries contrasts well with the nutty meringue.
SERVES 6–8

3 egg whites
175 g (6 oz) caster sugar
50 g (2 oz) hazelnuts, skinned, toasted and finely chopped
300 ml ($\frac{1}{2}$ pint) double cream
350 g (12 oz) fresh raspberries
icing sugar, for sifting
finely chopped pistachio nuts, for sprinkling

1. Line two baking sheets with non-stick baking paper, then draw a 20.5 cm (8 inch) circle on each one.

2. Whisk the egg whites until they are very stiff, but not dry. Adding just a little sugar at a time, gradually whisk the caster sugar into the egg whites, whisking well between each addition until the meringue is stiff and very shiny. Carefully fold in the chopped hazelnuts.

3. Divide the meringue equally between the two baking sheets, then spread neatly inside the rounds. With a palette knife, mark the top of one of the rounds into swirls—this will be the top of the gâteau.

4. Bake at 140°C (275°F) mark 1 for about $1\frac{1}{2}$ hours or until dry. Turn the oven off, and allow the meringues to cool in the oven.

5. Whip the cream until it will hold soft peaks. Carefully remove the meringues from the baking paper. Place the smooth meringue round on a large flat serving plate, then spread with the cream.

6. Arrange the raspberries on top of the cream, then place the second meringue on top. Sift icing sugar over the top of the gâteau, and sprinkle with finely chopped pistachio nuts. Serve as soon as possible.

French Apple Flan

As this flan is attributed to the apple-growing region of France, it is sometimes called Normandy Apple Flan. This recipe, which is just one of many versions, uses two types of apples, cooked in different ways, each one contrasting with the other.

SERVES 8

900 g (2 lb) cooking apples
175 g (6 oz) granulated sugar
50 g (2 oz) seedless raisins
60 ml (4 tbsp) Calvados
4–5 large dessert apples, e.g. Golden Delicious, Russet or Cox
50 g (2 oz) caster sugar
lightly whipped cream, to serve

FOR THE PÂTE SUCRÉE
150 g (5 oz) plain flour
pinch of salt
25 g (1 oz) icing sugar
75 g (3 oz) butter, diced
2 egg yolks

FOR THE GLAZE
175 g (6 oz) apricot conserve
15 ml (1 tbsp) Calvados

1. Peel, quarter, core and slice the cooking apples and put them in a large saucepan with the granulated sugar and 30 ml (2 tbsp) water. Cover and cook gently for about 20 minutes or until the apples become soft and fluffy.

2. Pour the cooked apples into a nylon sieve placed over a bowl and allow to drain and cool. (The apple juice will not be needed.)

3. Put the raisins into a small saucepan with the Calvados and cook gently for 2–3 minutes to soften the raisins. Allow to cool.

4. To make the pâte sucrée, sift the flour, salt and icing sugar into a bowl. Rub in the butter until the mixture resembles fine breadcrumbs. Add the egg yolks and mix with a round-bladed knife to form a dough. Turn on to a lightly floured surface and knead for a few seconds until smooth.

5. Roll out the pâte sucrée to a round 2.5 cm (1 inch) larger than a 25 cm (10 inch) fluted flan tin. Line the tin with the pastry, pressing it well into the flutes. Trim the edges.

6. Beat the cooked apples until fairly smooth, then fold in the raisins and Calvados. Spread the apple mixture evenly over the bottom of the pastry case.

7. Peel and core the dessert apples and cut each apple in half. Cut each half into thin slices.

8. Arrange the apple slices in concentric circles on top of the cooked apple mixture. Sprinkle the apple slices with caster sugar. Bake at 220°C (425°F) mark 7 for 30–35 minutes or until the pastry is cooked and the apple slices are tender and very lightly browned.

9. Meanwhile, to make the glaze, put the conserve into a small saucepan and heat gently, stirring all the time, until melted. Sieve the conserve through a nylon sieve and return to the pan. Add the Calvados and heat until boiling.

10. Immediately the flan is removed from the oven, brush the apricot glaze evenly over the apple slices. Allow the flan to cool to room temperature before serving. Serve with lightly whipped cream.

Right: French apple flan (above)

Tropical Pavlova

*The secret of a successful Pavlova is not to remove it
from the oven until it is cold—if taken out of the
oven while still hot, the sudden change in
temperature will cause it to crack.*

SERVES 6–8

4 egg whites

3.75 ml ($\frac{3}{4}$ tsp) cream of tartar

225 g (8 oz) caster sugar

5 ml (1 tsp) white vinegar

5 ml (1 tsp) vanilla essence

10 ml (2 tsp) cornflour

FOR THE DECORATION

450 ml ($\frac{3}{4}$ pint) double cream

5 ml (1 tsp) vanilla essence

1 ripe mango, peeled and diced

2 kiwi fruits, peeled and sliced

2 slices of fresh pineapple, peeled, cored and diced

1. Line a large baking sheet with non-stick baking paper. Whisk the egg whites with the cream of tartar until stiff, but not dry. Gradually whisk in the caster sugar, then quickly whisk in the vinegar, vanilla essence and cornflour.

2. Spoon the meringue into the centre of the lined baking sheet. Using a large palette knife, spread the meringue to form a smooth oval shape, about 23 cm (9 inches) long and 4 cm ($1\frac{1}{2}$ inches) deep. Bake at 140°C (275°F) mark 1 for $1\frac{1}{4}$ hours, then turn the oven off and leave the meringue in the oven until quite cold.

3. Transfer the meringue to a serving plate, carefully peeling off the paper.

4. Whip the cream with the vanilla essence until stiff, then spoon into a piping bag fitted with a medium star nozzle. Pipe shells of cream around the top edge of the Pavlova. Pipe a second ring of cream, leaving a gap between the rings.

5. Fill the gap with the prepared fruits. (If preferred, the cream may be spread on top of the Pavlova, with the fruits arranged in the centre.)

Chocolate Orange Soufflé

*Dark plain chocolate is the best kind to use for
mouth-watering desserts like this one, which call for
a good depth of flavour.*

SERVES 6–8

450 ml ($\frac{3}{4}$ pint) milk

175 g (6 oz) plain chocolate

3 eggs, separated, plus 1 egg white

75 g (3 oz) sugar

15 ml (1 tbsp) powdered gelatine

grated rind and juice of 1 orange

300 ml ($\frac{1}{2}$ pint) whipping cream

15 ml (1 tbsp) chocolate liqueur

1. Prepare a 900 ml ($1\frac{1}{2}$ pint) soufflé dish by cutting a double strip of greaseproof paper long enough to fit around the dish, and wide enough to stand 5 cm (2 inches) above the rim. Secure the collar firmly around the dish.

2. Put the milk in a saucepan and break 150 g (5 oz) of the chocolate into it. Heat gently until the chocolate melts, then cook over a high heat until almost boiling.

3. Whisk the egg yolks and sugar together until pale and thick. Gradually pour on the chocolate milk, stirring. Return to the saucepan and cook for about 20 minutes, stirring continuously, until the mixture is thick enough to coat the back of a wooden spoon. Do not boil.

4. Sprinkle the gelatine on to 45 ml (3 tbsp) water in a small heatproof bowl and leave to soften. Place the bowl over a saucepan of simmering water and stir until dissolved. Stir into the custard with the orange rind and juice. Cool.

5. Whip the cream until it just holds its shape, then fold most of the cream into the cold mixture, reserving a little for decorating. Whisk the egg whites until stiff and fold into the mixture.

6. Pour the mixture into the prepared dish and leave to set. Remove the paper collar.

7. Stir the liqueur into the remaining cream and use to decorate the soufflé. Grate the remaining chocolate and sprinkle on top.

Soufflé Pancakes with Blackberry Sauce

These little pancakes, filled with a tangy lemon mixture and served with a blackberry sauce, are quite delicious. A supply of pancakes and blackberry sauce in the freezer will make this a speedy dessert to prepare.
SERVES 4–8

50 g (2 oz) plain flour

pinch of salt

1 egg

150 ml ($\frac{1}{4}$ pint) milk

15 g ($\frac{1}{2}$ oz) unsalted butter, melted

15 ml (1 tbsp) brandy

butter, for frying

icing sugar, for sifting

FOR THE BLACKBERRY SAUCE
225 g (8 oz) fresh or frozen blackberries
50–75 g (2–3 oz) caster sugar

FOR THE SOUFFLÉ FILLING
2 egg yolks
50 g (2 oz) caster sugar
finely grated rind of 1 lemon
15 ml (1 tbsp) strained lemon juice
20 g ($\frac{3}{4}$ oz) plain flour, sifted
3 egg whites

1. Sift the flour and salt into a mixing bowl and make a well in the centre. Break in the egg, then gradually whisk into the flour, adding the milk as the mixture thickens. When the batter is smooth, mix in the melted butter and brandy. Cover and leave to stand for about 30 minutes.

2. Heat a little butter in a 15 cm (6 inch) heavy-based frying pan, then pour off any excess. Pour in just enough batter to cover the base of the pan thinly, and cook for about 1 minute or until the batter is set, and the pancake is lightly browned on the underside. Turn or toss the pancake and cook the other side for about 1 minute or until lightly browned.

3. Transfer the pancake to a plate and cover with a sheet of absorbent kitchen paper or greaseproof paper. Make seven more pancakes in the same way, placing paper between each one.

4. To make the sauce, work the blackberries through a nylon sieve into a small saucepan, then stir in the caster sugar to taste. Set aside until needed.

5. To make the soufflé filling, and complete the pancakes, butter a 31.5 × 25.5 cm (12$\frac{1}{2}$ × 10 inch) ovenproof dish. Whisk the egg yolks with half the caster sugar and the lemon rind until very thick, then whisk in the lemon juice. Fold in the flour. Whisk the egg whites until stiff, then gradually whisk in the remaining caster sugar, whisking until shiny. Fold the egg whites into the lemon mixture.

6. Spread the pancakes out on a work surface and divide the soufflé mixture equally between them, spooning it along the centre of each one. Bring the sides of each pancake up over the filling, until they just overlap.

7. Place the pancakes side-by-side in the buttered dish, sift lightly with icing sugar, then bake in the centre of the oven at 190°C (375°F) mark 5 for 12–15 minutes or until the soufflé mixture is well risen and lightly firm to the touch.

8. Meanwhile, heat the blackberry sauce and pour it into a warmed serving jug. Remove the cooked pancakes from the oven and sift lightly with more icing sugar. Serve immediately, with the hot blackberry sauce.

Christmas Pudding Ice Cream

All the nicest things that go into a Christmas pudding—dried fruit, rum, port and spices—are used in this unusual recipe.

SERVES 4–6

100 g (4 oz) mixed no-soak dried fruit
60 ml (4 tbsp) light or dark rum
30 ml (2 tbsp) port
grated rind and juice of 1 orange
450 ml ($\frac{3}{4}$ pint) single cream
3 egg yolks
100 g (4 oz) caster sugar
150 ml ($\frac{1}{4}$ pint) whipping cream
5 ml (1 tsp) ground mixed spice

1. Mix the dried fruit, rum, port and orange rind and juice together, then set aside to marinate overnight.

2. Gently heat the single cream to simmering point in a small saucepan.

3. Whisk the egg yolks and sugar together in a medium bowl until pale and thick. Gradually pour on the hot cream, stirring continuously.

4. Strain the mixture into a medium heavy-based or double saucepan and cook over a gentle heat, stirring continuously, for about 20 minutes or until the mixture is thick enough to coat the back of a wooden spoon. Do not boil. Set aside to cool.

5. Whip the whipping cream until stiff, then fold into the cold custard with the dried fruit mixture and mixed spice.

6. Pour into a shallow freezer container, then cover and freeze for 3 hours or until mushy.

7. Turn into a chilled bowl and beat well. Return to the freezer container and freeze for a further 2 hours.

8. Beat the mixture again, then turn into a 1.1 litre (2 pint) bombe mould, cover and freeze for a further 2 hours or until firm.

9. Transfer to the refrigerator for 30 minutes before serving. Turn on to a cold plate.

Squidgy Chocolate Roll

Chocoholics will love this rich recipe, which uses cocoa powder to flavour a moist sponge, rolled and filled with fresh cream. It is an ideal dinner party dessert.

SERVES 6–8

60 ml (4 tbsp) cocoa powder
150 ml ($\frac{1}{4}$ pint) milk
4 eggs, separated
100 g (4 oz) caster sugar
225 ml (8 fl oz) double cream
fresh strawberries and grated chocolate, to decorate

1. Grease and line a 20.5 × 30.5 cm (8 × 12 inch) Swiss roll tin. Mix the cocoa powder and milk in a small saucepan and heat gently until the cocoa powder has dissolved. Remove the pan from the heat and set aside to cool.

2. Whisk the egg yolks and sugar together until pale and fluffy. Whisk the cooled milk mixture into the egg yolk mixture.

3. Whisk the egg whites until stiff, then fold into the cocoa mixture. Spread the mixture evenly into the prepared tin and bake at 180°C (350°F) mark 4 for about 20 minutes or until the sponge has risen and is just firm to the touch.

4. Turn out on to a sheet of greaseproof paper and cover with a warm, damp tea-towel to prevent the sponge from drying out. Leave the sponge to cool for 20 minutes.

5. Meanwhile, whip the cream until stiff. Reserve half for decorating, and spread the remainder over the sponge. Roll it up carefully. Do not roll it up too tightly and do not worry if it cracks slightly.

6. Pipe the reserved cream on top and decorate with fresh strawberries and grated chocolate. Serve chilled.

Right: Christmas pudding ice cream (above)

Baked Apple and Coconut Pudding

Eating apples are sweeter than cookers and many varieties—especially Cox's—hold their shape well when cooked. Juicy slices are baked on top of a light and airy pudding mixture, and a topping of toasted coconut completes the dish.

SERVES 6

finely grated rind and juice of 1 lemon

100 g (4 oz) light soft brown sugar, plus 30 ml (2 tbsp)

6 medium eating apples, each weighing about 100 g (4 oz), peeled, cored and sliced

100 g (4 oz) butter, softened

2 eggs, separated

100 g (4 oz) plain wholemeal flour

7.5 ml (1½ tsp) baking powder

25 g (1 oz) desiccated coconut

about 60 ml (4 tbsp) apricot jam, warmed

shredded coconut, toasted, to decorate

1. Pour the lemon juice into a large bowl and stir in the 30 ml (2 tbsp) sugar. Add the apples, making sure they are well coated.

2. Gradually beat the 100 g (4 oz) sugar into the butter until well blended. Add the lemon rind, then beat in the egg yolks, one at a time. Stir in the flour, baking powder and desiccated coconut.

3. Whisk the egg whites until stiff but not dry, then fold into the creamed ingredients. Spoon into a lightly greased 23–25.5 cm (9–10 inch) fluted flan dish. Press the apples into the mixture, spooning any juices over them.

4. Stand the dish on a baking sheet and bake at 170°C (325°F) mark 3 for 1–1¼ hours or until well browned and firm to the touch, covering lightly with greaseproof paper if necessary.

5. Cool for about 15 minutes, then brush with the apricot jam and scatter over the toasted shredded coconut. Serve while still warm, with custard if liked.

Olde English Trifle

A perfect trifle should be a rich confection of fruit, light sponge, alcohol, real egg custard and whipped cream. The recipe has altered little over the centuries—at one time the custard was topped with syllabub, and fruit has not always been included.

SERVES 6–8

4 trifle sponges

60 ml (4 tbsp) cherry jam

15 ratafia biscuits

60 ml (4 tbsp) sherry

2 bananas

grated rind and juice of ½ lemon

225 g (8 oz) cherries, stoned

450 ml (¾ pint) milk

3 eggs

50 g (2 oz) caster sugar

150 ml (¼ pint) double cream

FOR THE DECORATION

glacé cherries

25 g (1 oz) chopped nuts, toasted

1. Cut the trifle sponges in half and spread with jam, then sandwich together. Arrange in the base of a glass serving dish.

2. Cover with ratafias and sprinkle with sherry. Peel and slice the bananas and coat in lemon juice. Arrange the bananas and cherries on top of the ratafias.

3. Heat the milk in a medium saucepan until almost boiling. In a large bowl, whisk together the eggs, lemon rind and sugar until pale, then pour on the hot milk, stirring continuously.

4. Return to the saucepan and heat gently for about 20 minutes, stirring continuously, until the custard thickens enough to coat the back of a wooden spoon. Do not allow to boil. Set aside to cool.

5. Pour the custard over the trifle and leave until cold.

6. Whip the cream until stiff and pipe on the top of the trifle. Decorate with glacé cherries and chopped nuts.

Vanilla Soufflé with Pistachio Nuts

This very light creamy soufflé, decorated with pistachio nuts, can be made a day in advance.

SERVES 8

20 ml (4 tsp) powdered gelatine

6 eggs, separated

175 g (6 oz) caster sugar

10 ml (2 tsp) vanilla essence

450 ml ($\frac{3}{4}$ pint) double cream

25 g (1 oz) pistachio nuts, skinned and chopped

whole pistachio nuts, to decorate

1. Prepare a 1.4 litre (2$\frac{1}{2}$ pint) soufflé dish by cutting a double strip of greaseproof paper long enough to fit around the dish, and wide enough to stand 5 cm (2 inches) above the rim. Secure the collar firmly and place the dish on a flat plate.

2. Sprinkle the gelatine over 60 ml (4 tbsp) water in a small heatproof bowl and leave for 2 minutes to soften. Stand the bowl over a saucepan of hot water and heat gently, stirring, until the gelatine dissolves.

3. Whisk the egg yolks with the caster sugar and vanilla until they are very thick and will hold a ribbon trail.

4. Whip 300 ml ($\frac{1}{2}$ pint) of the cream until it just holds soft peaks. Whisk the egg whites until they are very stiff.

5. Whisk the hot gelatine into the egg yolks, then fold in the whipped cream. Very carefully, and quickly, fold in the egg whites. Pour the soufflé mixture into the prepared dish and chill for at least 2 hours, or until set.

6. When set, carefully remove the paper collar. Coat the sides of the soufflé with the chopped nuts.

7. Whip the remaining cream until thick. Spoon into a small piping bag fitted with a small star nozzle and pipe rosettes around the top edge of the soufflé. Decorate with pistachio nuts. Chill until ready to serve.

Cherries in Brandy

A simple way to serve cherries, which shows them off at their best, steeped in a spicy alcoholic syrup and accompanied by a light orange cream. For easy eating, stone the cherries first, using a special cherry stoner or a skewer.

SERVES 6

900 g (2 lb) cherries, stoned

15 g ($\frac{1}{2}$ oz) sugar

1 cinnamon stick

finely grated rind and juice of 2 oranges

30 ml (2 tbsp) redcurrant jelly

60 ml (4 tbsp) cherry brandy or brandy

150 ml ($\frac{1}{4}$ pint) double cream

150 ml ($\frac{1}{4}$ pint) natural yogurt

1. Place the cherries in a saucepan with the sugar, cinnamon, half of the orange rind and the juice of both oranges. Cover and cook over a low heat for about 10 minutes or until the cherries are soft and the juice runs.

2. Stir in the redcurrant jelly and the brandy and cook gently until the jelly melts. Cool, then chill.

3. Mix the remaining orange rind and the cream together in a bowl. Whip until the cream just holds its shape, then fold in the yogurt. Serve the cherries in brandy, with the orange cream handed separately.

The Perfect Fresh Fruit Salad

Fruit salad can be made with a single fruit, or with a mixture of an indefinite number, according to availability. Use as many fruits as are available, so that the flavours can intermingle to make a highly perfumed salad, as in this recipe. Do not use bananas in a fruit salad; their very strong flavour will dominate and spoil the overall taste.

SERVES 12

450 g (1 lb) granulated sugar
thinly pared rind and strained juice of 1 lemon
2 large dessert apples
3 large pears, peeled
1 small pineapple, skin and core removed, cut into small slices
1 small ripe melon, seeds removed, flesh removed with a melon baller
3 large oranges, skin and all white pith removed, cut into segments
100 g (4 oz) black grapes, halved and seeded
100 g (4 oz) green grapes, halved and seeded
225 g (8 oz) dark sweet cherries, stoned
225 g (8 oz) dessert plums, skinned, stoned and sliced
1 large ripe mango, peeled and thinly sliced
3 large peaches, skinned, stoned and thinly sliced
225 g (8 oz) strawberries, hulled and sliced
225 g (8 oz) raspberries
3 kiwi fruit, peeled and sliced
lightly whipped cream, to serve

1. Put the sugar and lemon rind in a large saucepan with 600 ml (1 pint) water. Heat gently until the sugar has dissolved, then bring to the boil and boil for 5 minutes. Stir in the lemon juice and allow to cool.
2. Remove the rind from the syrup, then pour into a bowl.
3. Quarter, core and thinly slice the apples and pears. Add them to the syrup, then stir in the other fruits. Mix the salad gently, then cover the surface with cling film and chill. Serve with whipped cream.

Strawberry Mousses

These mousses can be made a day ahead and kept, covered, in the refrigerator.

SERVES 4

450 g (1 lb) strawberries, hulled
15 ml (1 tbsp) powdered gelatine
100 g (4 oz) caster sugar
10 ml (2 tsp) lemon juice
225 ml (8 fl oz) whipping cream
2 egg whites

FOR THE DECORATION
sliced strawberries
Cognac
fresh mint leaves, cut into strips

1. Purée the strawberries in a blender or food processor, then pass through a sieve to remove the seeds.
2. Dissolve the gelatine in a little of the purée in a small bowl placed over a saucepan of hot water. Remove from the heat and allow to cool slightly, then blend with the remaining purée. Add half the sugar and lemon juice to taste.
3. Whip the cream and fold into the purée. Whisk the egg whites until stiff but not dry, then gradually whisk in half the remaining sugar. Add the rest of the sugar and whisk until stiff. Fold into the purée.
4. Divide the mousse equally between four lightly oiled ramekin dishes and leave to set in a cold place. Cover loosely with cling film when set.
5. For the decoration, sprinkle the sliced strawberries with a little Cognac and mint and chill.
6. To serve, unmould the mousses on to cold plates and decorate with the strawberries sprinkled with Cognac and mint.

Right: Marbled chocolate teabread (page 116)

Afternoon Tea

Marbled Chocolate Teabread

This recipe is so called because the swirls of chocolate make a pattern similar to Italian marble.
MAKES ABOUT 10 SLICES

225 g (8 oz) butter, softened

225 g (8 oz) caster sugar

4 eggs, beaten

225 g (8 oz) self-raising flour

finely grated rind of 1 large orange

15 ml (1 tbsp) orange juice

few drops of orange-flower water (optional)

75 g (3 oz) plain chocolate

15 ml (1 tbsp) cocoa powder

1. Grease a 900 ml (2 pint) loaf tin and line the base and sides with greaseproof paper.
2. Cream the butter and sugar together until pale and fluffy, then gradually beat in the eggs, beating well after each addition. Fold in the flour.
3. Transfer half the mixture to another bowl and beat in the orange rind, juice and orange-flower water, if using.
4. Break the chocolate into pieces, put into a small heatproof bowl and place over a pan of simmering water. Stir until the chocolate melts. Stir into the remaining cake mixture with the cocoa powder.
5. Put alternate spoonfuls of the two mixtures into the prepared tin. Use a knife to swirl through the mixture to make a marbled effect, then level the surface.
6. Bake at 180°C (350°F) mark 4 for $1\frac{1}{4}$–$1\frac{1}{2}$ hours or until well risen and firm to the touch. Turn out on to a wire rack to cool. Serve cut in slices.

Two-tier Gooey Chocolate Cake

The secret of melting chocolate successfully is not to let it get too hot. Always melt chocolate in a bowl over a pan of hot water, not directly in the pan itself, making sure that the bottom of the bowl does not touch the water.
MAKES 12 SLICES

FOR THE BOTTOM LAYER

225 g (8 oz) plain dessert chocolate pieces

15 ml (1 tbsp) rum

5 eggs, separated

150 g (5 oz) caster sugar

100 g (4 oz) unsalted butter, diced

FOR THE TOP LAYER

225 g (8 oz) plain dessert chocolate pieces

30 ml (2 tbsp) rum

4 eggs, separated

FOR THE DECORATION

grated chocolate

blanched shreds of orange rind

1. Grease a 20.5 cm (8 inch) springform tin and line with greaseproof paper. Grease the paper.
2. To make the bottom layer of the cake, place the chocolate in a heatproof bowl over a pan of simmering water. Heat gently until the chocolate melts, stirring once or twice. Stir the rum into the chocolate and remove the bowl from the heat.
3. Put the egg yolks and sugar in a bowl and whisk with an electric beater until thick and creamy. Beat in the butter, a little at a time, until smooth. Beat in the melted chocolate until smooth.

4. In a separate clean bowl, whisk the egg whites until stiff, then fold into the chocolate mixture. Turn into the prepared tin. Bake at 180°C (350°F) mark 4 for 40 minutes or until risen and firm. Leave the cake to cool in the tin for 1 hour.

5. To make the top layer of the cake, melt the chocolate and stir in the rum, as for the bottom layer. Remove the bowl from the heat, cool for 1–2 minutes, then beat in the egg yolks. Whisk the egg whites until stiff, as before, and fold into the chocolate mixture.

6. Press the crust down on the baked cake with your fingers. Pour the top layer over the cake in the tin. Chill in the refrigerator overnight.

7. To serve, remove the cake carefully from the tin. Sprinkle grated chocolate around the edge and decorate with shreds of orange rind.

Mille-feuilles

Translated, mille-feuille means a thousand leaves. Mille-feuille is made up of layers of puff pastry sandwiched together with crème pâtissière. Classic mille-feuille is made up of round layers of pastry, but it can also be made with oblong layers, which are easier to handle.
MAKES 8 SLICES

368 g (13 oz) packet frozen puff pastry, thawed

45 ml (3 tbsp) raspberry conserve

175 g (6 oz) icing sugar, sifted

30 ml (2 tbsp) boiling water

40 g (1½ oz) almonds, blanched, toasted and finely chopped

FOR THE CRÈME PÂTISSIÈRE

3 egg yolks

50 g (2 oz) caster sugar

35 g (1¼ oz) plain flour, sifted

300 ml (½ pint) milk

5 ml (1 tsp) vanilla essence

1 egg white

150 ml (¼ pint) double cream

1. Roll out the pastry on a lightly floured surface to a rectangle 33 × 38 cm (13 × 15 inches). Trim the pastry edges neatly, then prick the pastry well with a fork.

2. Cut the pastry into three oblongs, each one 12.5 × 33 cm (5 × 13 inches). Place the pastry strips on baking sheets and chill for 30 minutes.

3. Meanwhile, to make the crème pâtissière, whisk the egg yolks with 15 g (½ oz) caster sugar in a bowl until pale and thick. Fold in the flour.

4. Put the milk and the vanilla in a saucepan and bring almost to the boil. Gently whisk the hot milk into the egg and flour mixture. Strain the mixture back into the pan.

5. Cook the custard over a gentle heat, stirring, until the mixture thickens. Turn the custard into a bowl and leave to cool completely.

6. Whisk the egg white until stiff, then whisk in the remaining sugar. Whip the cream until thick. Whisk the cooled custard, then gradually fold in the egg white, followed by the cream.

7. Dampen the baking sheets around the pastry strips with a little cold water. Bake at 230°C (450°F) mark 8 for 25–30 minutes or until well risen and golden brown. Cool the pastry strips on a wire rack.

8. Place the puff pastry strips one on top of the other and trim the sides neatly. Choose the most even layer for the top, turning it upside down if necessary to make a flat surface.

9. Place the bottom layer on a serving dish and spread with half of the crème pâtissière and half the jam. Place the second pastry layer on top and spread with the remaining jam and crème pâtissière, then place the last layer of pastry on top with the flat side uppermost.

10. Mix the icing sugar with the hot water to form an icing thick enough to coat the back of the spoon—do not make it too thin. Spread the icing evenly over the top layer of pastry and immediately sprinkle it with the chopped almonds. Allow the icing to set. Serve cut into eight slices.

Carrot Cake

Root vegetables were often used to lend sweetness to 18th-century cakes and puddings. Beetroots, parsnips and carrots were all common ingredients, but of these, only carrot is still favoured today. It makes a very pleasant, moist cake, without any hint of carrot in the taste.

SERVES 8

225 g (8 oz) butter, softened

225 g (8 oz) light soft brown sugar

4 eggs, separated

finely grated rind of ½ orange

20 ml (4 tsp) lemon juice

175 g (6 oz) self-raising flour

5 ml (1 tsp) baking powder

50 g (2 oz) ground almonds

150 g (5 oz) walnut pieces, chopped

350 g (12 oz) young carrots, peeled and grated

225 g (8 oz) cream cheese

10 ml (2 tsp) clear honey

1. Grease and line a deep 20.5 cm (8 inch) round cake tin.

2. Cream the butter and sugar together in a bowl until pale and fluffy. Beat in the egg yolks, then stir in the orange rind and 15 ml (3 tsp) of the lemon juice.

3. Sift in the flour and baking powder, then stir in the ground almonds and 100 g (4 oz) of the walnuts.

4. Whisk the egg whites until stiff, then fold into the cake mixture with the carrots. Pour into the prepared tin and hollow the centre slightly.

5. Bake at 180°C (350°F) mark 4 for about 1½ hours. Cover the top with foil after 1 hour if it starts to brown.

6. Leave to cool slightly, then turn out on to a wire rack and remove the lining paper. Leave to cool.

7. To make the topping, beat together the cheese, honey and remaining lemon juice and spread over the top of the cake. Sprinkle the topping with the remaining walnuts.

Cherry and Almond Cake

Ground almonds give an unbeatably moist texture and delicate flavour to this cake, and juicy glacé cherries make it even more tempting. Don't buy too large a quantity of ground almonds at a time, as they quickly lose flavour once the pack is opened.

MAKES ABOUT 12 SLICES

275 g (10 oz) glacé cherries

225 g (8 oz) butter, softened

225 g (8 oz) caster sugar

6 eggs, beaten

65 g (2½ oz) self-raising flour

pinch of salt

175 g (6 oz) ground almonds

2.5 ml (½ tsp) almond flavouring

icing sugar, to decorate

1. Grease a deep 23 cm (9 inch) loose-bottomed round cake tin and line the base and sides with greaseproof paper. Grease the paper.

2. Arrange the cherries in the bottom of the tin.

3. Cream the butter and sugar together until pale and fluffy. Beat in the eggs, a little at a time, adding a little of the flour if the mixture shows signs of curdling.

4. Sift in the remaining flour and salt, then add the ground almonds and almond flavouring.

5. Turn the mixture into the prepared tin and bake at 180°C (350°F) mark 4 for 1 hour or until firm to the touch. Cover with greaseproof paper if browning too quickly. Leave in the tin to cool.

6. When the cake is cold, remove from the tin and dredge the top with icing sugar.

Right: Cherry and almond cake (above)

Glazed Fruit Tartlets

You can use any shape of mould for these tartlets, as long as their capacity is roughly the same. Different fruits can be used instead of the strawberries, or you can use a mixture of fruits, such as halved grapes, whole raspberries, sliced peaches or kiwi.

MAKES 12

100 g (4 oz) plain flour

pinch of salt

50 g (2 oz) butter

50 g (2 oz) caster sugar

2 egg yolks

few drops of vanilla essence

75 ml (5 tbsp) redcurrant jelly

juice of ½ lemon

225 g (8 oz) strawberries, hulled and sliced

1. Sift the flour and salt into a large bowl. Rub the butter into the flour until the mixture resembles fine breadcrumbs. Stir in the sugar.

2. Make a well in the centre of the mixture and add the egg yolks and vanilla essence. Mix quickly with a knife, then gather together with the fingertips and knead very lightly to make a smooth ball of dough. Chill in the refrigerator for about 30 minutes.

3. Roll out the dough thinly on a lightly floured surface and use to line twelve 100 ml (4 fl oz) individual moulds. Prick with a skewer, then chill in the refrigerator for 15 minutes.

4. Line the dough with foil and fill with baking beans. Bake blind at 190°C (375°F) mark 5 for 15 minutes. Remove the foil and beans, then return to the oven for 3–5 minutes or until the pastry is golden and crisp. Leave the pastry cases to cool in the moulds for a few minutes, before removing.

5. Melt the redcurrant jelly with the lemon juice. Brush over the inside of the pastry cases and immediately arrange the strawberries in the cases. Brush with the remaining glaze. Leave until set before serving.

Hazelnut Cartwheel

Hazelnuts are found in many parts of the world and are also called cob nuts or filberts. As well as being useful for lending crunch and flavour to recipes like this, hazelnuts are good on their own, as a healthy snack, or as an accompaniment to wine and cheese.

SERVES 8

225 g (8 oz) packet frozen puff pastry, thawed

25 g (1 oz) butter, softened

25 g (1 oz) light soft brown sugar

1 egg, beaten

75 g (3 oz) plain cake crumbs

75 g (3 oz) hazelnuts, chopped

50 g (2 oz) seedless raisins

finely grated rind of 1 lemon

1 egg, beaten, to glaze

caster sugar, to dredge

1. Roll out the pastry on a lightly floured surface to a rectangle about 40.5 × 25.5 cm (16 × 10 inches).

2. Cream the butter and sugar together until pale and fluffy, then beat in the egg and stir in the cake crumbs, hazelnuts, raisins and lemon rind. Spread the mixture over the pastry to within 0.5 cm (¼ inch) of the edges.

3. Roll up like a Swiss roll, starting from the narrow end. Trim the ends, if necessary.

4. Place on a dampened baking sheet and curl round into a circle. Seal the ends together.

5. Snip all round the ring at 4 cm (1½ inch) intervals so the cuts come to within about 2 cm (¾ inch) of the ring's inner edge. Brush with beaten egg to glaze. Bake at 220°C (425°F) mark 7 for 25–30 minutes or until golden brown. Dredge with sugar and serve warm.

Potato Scones

These scones need to be made from floury potatoes such as Pentland Squire or Maris Piper which will mash well. You can use leftover cooked potatoes, but for the best flavour, boil them freshly.

MAKES ABOUT 12

450 g (1 lb) floury potatoes, peeled

5 ml (1 tsp) salt

25 g (1 oz) butter

about 100 g (4 oz) plain flour

1. Cook the potatoes in boiling salted water for about 20 minutes or until tender. Drain and mash until smooth. Add the salt and butter while the potatoes are still hot, then work in enough flour to make a stiff dough.

2. Turn on to a floured surface, knead lightly and roll out until 0.5 cm ($\frac{1}{4}$ inch) thick. Cut into about 12 rounds with a 6.5 cm ($2\frac{1}{2}$ inch) cutter.

3. Cook on a greased griddle or heavy-based frying pan for 4–5 minutes on each side or until golden brown. Serve hot with butter.

Petticoat Tails

These traditional Scottish shortbread biscuits date back beyond the 12th century. The triangles fit together into a circle and were the same shape as the pieces of fabric used to make a full-gored petticoat in Elizabethan times.

MAKES 8

100 g (4 oz) butter, softened

50 g (2 oz) caster sugar, plus extra for dredging

150 g (5 oz) plain flour

50 g (2 oz) ground rice

1. In a medium bowl, cream the butter and sugar together until pale and fluffy.

2. Gradually stir in the flour and ground rice. Draw the mixture together and press into an 18 cm (7 inch) round sandwich tin.

3. Prick well all over and pinch up the edges with a finger and thumb. Mark into eight triangles with a sharp knife. Bake at 170°C (325°F) mark 3 for about 40 minutes or until pale straw in colour.

4. Leave in the tin for 5 minutes, then cut into triangles. Dredge with caster sugar. Remove from the tin when cold. Store in an airtight container.

Orange Curd Cake

This cake can be made the day before serving and kept covered in a cool place.

MAKES ONE 23 cm (9 inch) CAKE

450 g (1 lb) ricotta cheese, sieved

175 g (6 oz) caster sugar

25 g (1 oz) semolina

4 eggs, separated

45 ml (3 tbsp) orange juice

10 ml (2 tsp) finely grated orange rind

50 g (2 oz) candied peel, chopped

1. Grease a 23 cm (9 inch) loose-bottomed cake tin.

2. Beat the cheese, sugar, semolina, egg yolks and orange juice and rind together. Stir in the peel. Whisk the egg whites until stiff, but not dry, then carefully fold into the cheese mixture until just evenly blended.

3. Spoon into the prepared tin and bake at 180°C (350°F) mark 4 for 30–35 minutes or until just set in the centre.

4. Leave the cake to cool slightly in the tin before removing it, still on the base of the tin. Carefully slide the cake from the base on to a wire rack covered by a sheet of greaseproof paper, so that it remains the right way up. Leave to cool.

Butter Biscuits

You may need to go to an ethnic food shop to buy ready-ground cardamom. An alternative is to buy cardamom pods, to remove the seeds and grind them yourself.
MAKES 15–20

225 g (8 oz) plain flour
pinch of salt
1.25 ml (¼ tsp) baking powder
7.5 ml (1½ tsp) ground cardamom
175 g (6 oz) unsalted butter, diced
75 g (3 oz) icing sugar
2.5 ml (½ tsp) vanilla essence

FOR THE GLACÉ ICING WITH COGNAC
50 g (2 oz) icing sugar
10–15 ml (2–3 tsp) Cognac

1. Sift the flour, salt, baking powder and cardamom into a bowl. Rub in the butter until the mixture resembles breadcrumbs.
2. Sift the icing sugar over, then gently stir in. Sprinkle the vanilla essence over, then press the ingredients together to make a smooth dough. Cover and chill for at least 3 hours.
3. Roll out the dough on a lightly floured surface, using a lightly floured rolling pin, to about 0.5 cm (¼ inch) thick. Cut into rounds with a floured 6.5 cm (2½ inch) fluted cutter. Transfer to baking sheets, leaving about 1 cm (½ inch) space around each.
4. Bake at 190°C (375°F) mark 5 for about 12 minutes or until lightly golden. Leave to set on the baking sheets for a few minutes, then transfer to a wire rack to cool.
5. To make the glacé icing, sift the icing sugar and mix to a smooth consistency with about 5 ml (1 tsp) cold water and the Cognac. Spread a thin layer over the tops of the biscuits. Leave to set.

Walnut Clusters

In this recipe, walnuts are combined with chocolate to produce small, crunchy, mounded biscuits. The walnuts can be replaced by other nuts, such as almonds or hazelnuts, to vary the flavour.
MAKES ABOUT 36

40 g (1½ oz) plain chocolate
50 g (2 oz) butter
100 g (4 oz) caster sugar
1 egg, beaten
7.5 ml (1½ tsp) vanilla essence
50 g (2 oz) plain flour
2.5 ml (½ tsp) salt
1.25 ml (¼ tsp) baking powder
175 g (6 oz) walnut pieces, chopped
icing sugar, for dredging

1. Grease and line three baking sheets with rice paper. Break the chocolate into pieces and put in a heatproof bowl over a saucepan of simmering water. Heat gently until the chocolate has melted. Leave to cool slightly.
2. Cream the butter with the sugar and chocolate until fluffy. Beat in the egg and vanilla essence. Sift in the flour, salt and baking powder and fold into the butter mixture with the walnuts.
3. Drop heaped teaspoonfuls of the mixture well apart on to the prepared baking sheets.
4. Bake at 180°C (350°F) mark 4 for 10 minutes. Transfer to a wire rack and leave to cool. Dredge with icing sugar.

Right: Petticoat tails (page 121), butter biscuits (above), walnut clusters (above)

Griddle Pancakes

Today's cookers make cooking on a griddle much less of a hit-and-miss business than when the griddle or bakestone was perched over the coals of the fire. These pancakes, or 'drop scones', should be eaten as soon as they are cooked. They are quick and easy to make but don't reheat well.

MAKES 15–18

100 g (4 oz) self-raising flour
30 ml (2 tbsp) caster sugar
1 egg, beaten
150 ml ($\frac{1}{4}$ pint) milk

1. Mix the flour and sugar. Make a well in the centre and stir in the egg, with enough of the milk to make a batter the consistency of thick cream. The mixing should be done as quickly and lightly as possible.
2. Drop the mixture in spoonfuls on to a greased hot griddle or heavy-based frying pan. For round pancakes, drop it from the point of the spoon; for oval ones, drop from the side.
3. Keep the griddle at a steady heat and when bubbles rise to the surface of the pancakes and burst, after 2–3 minutes, turn the pancakes over with a palette knife. Continue cooking for a further 2–3 minutes or until golden brown on the other side.
4. Wrap the cooked pancakes in a clean tea-towel to keep them warm. Repeat with the remaining mixture to make 15–18 pancakes. Serve while still warm with butter or with golden syrup or honey.

Brandy Snaps

Brandy snaps can be kept, unfilled, in an airtight container for up to a week.

MAKES ABOUT 12

50 g (2 oz) butter
50 g (2 oz) caster sugar
30 ml (2 tbsp) golden syrup
50 g (2 oz) plain flour
2.5 ml ($\frac{1}{2}$ tsp) ground ginger
5 ml (1 tsp) brandy
finely grated rind of $\frac{1}{2}$ lemon
150 ml ($\frac{1}{4}$ pint) double cream

1. Line two or three large baking sheets with non-stick baking paper.
2. Gently heat the butter, sugar and syrup in a saucepan until the butter has melted and the sugar dissolved. Remove from the heat.
3. Sift the flour and ginger together, then stir into the melted mixture with the brandy and lemon rind.
4. Drop teaspoons of the mixture on to the prepared baking sheets, leaving 10 cm (4 inches) between each one. Bake at 180°C (350°F) mark 4 for 7 minutes or until cooked.
5. Quickly remove the biscuits from the baking sheets, using a palette knife. Roll each one around the buttered handle of a wooden spoon. Leave on the handles until set, then gently twist to remove. Cool on a wire rack.
6. If the biscuits set before they have been shaped, return them to the oven for a few minutes to soften. Store in an airtight container until required.
7. Just before serving, whip the cream until it just holds its shape. Spoon into a piping bag fitted with a star nozzle and pipe cream into the ends of the snaps. Serve immediately.

Pinwheel Sandwiches

Two small loaves make what seems to be an enormous number of pinwheels, but as they are dainty and bite-sized, most people can eat quite a few and there is no point in making less. Very fresh bread is an absolute must for making pinwheels successfully. If the bread is not fresh, it will not roll without cracking.

MAKES ABOUT 84

105 g (4 oz) can red salmon

175 g (6 oz) full-fat soft cheese

30–60 ml (2–4 tbsp) thick mayonnaise

5 ml (1 tsp) lemon juice

1.25 ml ($\frac{1}{4}$ tsp) cayenne pepper

salt

2 eggs, hard-boiled, shelled and finely chopped

45–60 ml (3–4 tbsp) finely chopped fresh watercress or parsley

2.5 ml ($\frac{1}{2}$ tsp) French mustard

freshly ground black pepper

1 very fresh small white sandwich loaf

1 very fresh small wholemeal sandwich loaf

75–100 g (3–4 oz) butter, softened

1. Drain the salmon. Flake the flesh in a bowl, discarding the skin and any bones, then mash finely. Add half the soft cheese, 15–30 ml (1–2 tbsp) mayonnaise, the lemon juice, cayenne pepper and salt to taste. Beat with a wooden spoon until well combined.

2. Put the remaining cheese in a separate bowl with the chopped eggs, 15–30 ml (1–2 tbsp) mayonnaise, the watercress or parsley, mustard and salt and pepper to taste. Beat with a wooden spoon until well combined.

3. Cut the crusts off all sides of the loaves, except the bases, to make a squared-off shape. Turn each loaf on its side and, holding the base, cut lengthways into seven thick slices. Discard the base crust. Spread one side of each slice with butter.

4. Spread the white bread with the egg filling and the brown bread with the salmon. Roll up each slice from one short end, then wrap each one individually in cling film. Chill in the refrigerator for 2–4 hours or until firm.

5. To serve, unwrap and cut each roll into six slices. Arrange on a serving plate.

Cheese and Chive Scones

Crumbly Lancashire cheese is ideal in cooking. Combined with the onion flavour of freshly snipped chives, these scones are deliciously savoury.

MAKES 10

225 g (8 oz) self-raising flour

pinch of salt

50 g (2 oz) butter, diced

100 g (4 oz) Lancashire cheese, grated

15 ml (1 tbsp) snipped fresh chives

150 ml ($\frac{1}{4}$ pint) milk, plus extra for brushing

1. Put the flour and salt into a bowl and rub in the butter until the mixture resembles fine breadcrumbs. Stir in 50 g (2 oz) of the cheese and the chives.

2. Add the milk and mix to form a soft dough, then knead quickly until smooth.

3. Roll out on a floured surface until 1 cm ($\frac{1}{2}$ inch) thick. Cut into 10 rounds with a 5 cm (2 inch) plain cutter and brush the tops with milk. Transfer to baking sheets.

4. Bake at 230°C (450°F) mark 8 for 7–10 minutes or until well risen and golden brown.

5. Immediately sprinkle the remaining cheese on top of the scones and allow to melt before serving hot or cold.

Overleaf: Two-tier gooey chocolate cake (page 116), glazed fruit tartlets (page 120), pinwheel sandwiches (above)

PORTMEIRION

INDEX